Series/Number 07-088

WORKING WITH ARCHIVAL DATA
Studying Lives

GLEN H. ELDER, Jr.
University of North Carolina at Chapel Hill

ELIZA K. PAVALKO
Indiana University

ELIZABETH C. CLIPP
Duke University

SAGE Publications
International Educational and Professional Publisher
Newbury Park   London   New Delhi

For information address:

SAGE Publications, Inc.
2455 Teller Road
Newbury Park, California 91320
E-mail: order@sagepub.com

SAGE Publications Ltd.
6 Bonhill Street
London EC2A 4PU
United Kingdom

SAGE Publications India Pvt. Ltd.
M-32 Market
Greater Kailash I
New Delhi 110 048 India

Printed in the United States of America

Elder, Glen H., Jr.
    Working with archival data: studying lives / Glen H. Elder, Jr., Eliza
K. Pavalko, Elizabeth C. Clipp.
        p.   cm.—(Quantitative applications in the social sciences; 88)
    Includes bibliographical references (p.   ).
    ISBN 0-8039-4262-1 (pb)
    1. Social sciences—Research. 2. Longitudinal method. 3. Social sciences—Information
services. I. Pavalko, Eliza K. II. Clipp, Elizabeth C. (Elizabeth Colerick) III. Title.
IV. Series: Sage university papers series. Quantitative applications in the social sciences; 88.
    H62.E465 1993   92-30713
    400′.72—dc20   CIP

                99 00 01 10 9 8 7 6 5 4

Sage Production Editor: Tara S. Mead

When citing a university paper, please use the proper form. Remember to cite the current Sage University Paper series title and include the paper number. One of the following formats can be adapted (depending on the style manual used):

(1) ELDER, G. H., Jr., PAVALKO, E. K., and CLIPP, E. C. (1992) Working With Archival Data: Studying Lives. Sage University Paper series on Quantitative Applications in the Social Sciences, 07-088. Newbury Park, CA: Sage.

OR

(2) Elder, G. H., Jr., Pavalko, E. K., & Clipp, E. C. (1992) *Working with archival data: Studying lives* (Sage University Paper series on Quantitative Applications in the Social Sciences, series no. 07-088). Newbury Park, CA: Sage.

CONTENTS

SERIES EDITOR'S INTRODUCTION

During the 1960s, a number of major longitudinal studies were launched, such as the Michigan Panel Study of Income Dynamics, Project Talent, and the National Longitudinal Surveys. Take the first example, the Michigan Panel of more than 6,000 families. From this study came a surprising discovery: Poverty is an enduring condition (i.e., lasts beyond a year) for very few people. This finding, which undid a popular myth, was made possible by the longitudinal nature of the study, which has aimed to reinterview the same families every year since 1968. However, valuable as the Michigan Panel is, it was designed to study neither the life course nor the influences of major historical events on that life course. If researchers wish to "study lives" with these data, they are forced to recast them, or, failing that, to turn to other archival data.

This is what Professor Elder and his colleagues are about as they "ask new questions of old data." They examine original materials gathered for other purposes, in other longitudinal studies, and shape those materials into observations relevant for their research on individual lives. In explicating the method, they utilize throughout the well-known Lewis Terman Study, begun in 1921 to track a sample of gifted young people (857 boys and 671 girls) across 10 years. Since that time, there have been 12 additional interview waves, the most recent in 1991. The data archives on the Terman Study contain, besides the interviews themselves, considerable supplementary information, such as newspaper stories, spouse and parent interviews, and letters. The authors describe the steps they follow in order to "recast the archive": evaluate existing materials, decide on recoding, refine the research questions, evaluate the coding schemes, write the codebook, code the case, assess reliability and validity, conduct data analysis. They illustrate this process in the construction of new health codes (Chapter 3), career patterns (Chapter 4), and measures of the influence of World War II (Chapter 5).

The extended attention to the Terman Study is useful, for it shows the power of the method. Of course, the method could serve equally well if applied to other longitudinal data sets. If the reader does not have one in mind, he or she may be stimulated by the several additional archival sources the authors mention. Moreover, as they note in the appendix, almost 200 longitudinal data sets are available from a national repository, the Henry A. Murray Research Center. Thus the sort of rich analysis presented here can be carried out on many other research topics.

—Michael S. Lewis-Beck
Series Editor

ACKNOWLEDGMENTS

Some books owe their existence to their authors' lifetime of associations and professional experiences. This is such a monograph, for it conveys the way we have used archival data to investigate questions regarding the life course in changing societies. This approach has evolved over the past 30 years from informal understandings to the stepwise method outlined in the chapters that follow. The National Institute of Mental Health has generously supported the research from the late 1960s to the present.

The initial procedures were developed by the senior author in the course of a program of work with longitudinal data archives at the Institute of Human Development, University of California, Berkeley. We are indebted to the pioneering directors of these studies, to Harold E. Jones and Herbert Stolz of the Oakland Growth Study as well as the leadership of Mary Jones and John A. Clausen; and to Jean MacFarlane and Marjorie Honzik of the Berkeley Guidance Study. The rich data of these studies provided fertile ground for thinking through ways of fitting new research questions to old data. The Institute of Human Development could not have been more encouraging of these efforts, and we are grateful for the support of its directors over the years: John A. Clausen, Paul Mussen, M. Brewster Smith, Guy Swanson, and Joe Campos.

During the cold winter months of 1983 at Cornell University, the senior investigator discovered the potential usefulness of the longitudinal Lewis Terman Study for a study of war's legacy in men's lives. We explored these possibilities more deeply and launched at mid-decade a study of military service in World War II and its effects on adult development and aging. The late Robert Sears, then director of the Terman Study, had devoted substantial resources to coding the data and expressed particular interest in and support for the study we proposed. But little did he (or we, for that matter) know how many times we would be returning to work in the data archive. We could not have completed the arduous task of recasting the data for new research purposes without

viii

the steadfast support of Sears, the archivist Eleanor Walker, and Al
Hastorf, current director. A grant from the National Institute of Mental
Health (MH 41327) and a Merit Review Grant from the Veterans
Administration enabled us to carry out this research venture. For all of
this support, we are deeply grateful.

The successful implementation of our objectives in recasting the
Terman data on men is due primarily to the superb leadership of
Catherine Cross, programmer and project manager, who brought a high
level of expertise on coding to the enterprise. Working with us, she
played a key role in preparing the codebooks with painstaking care and
in training the coders. She was ably assisted on the home-front mobilization coding by Andrew Workman, an advanced graduate student in
history at UNC-Chapel Hill. We have been most fortunate in the excep-
tional thoughtfulness and thoroughness of our coders, Karen Catoe,
Marty Williams Deane, Laura Kline, and Michael Riddle. Joyce Tabor
skillfully directs the coding unit at the Carolina Population Center. We
are deeply indebted to them, and to the editorial skills of Lynn Igoe.
Collectively, they made this research operation more manageable and
successful than we could ever have hoped for. As a token of our
appreciation for their work, we dedicate this volume to everyone who
played a role in the all-important coding operations of this study.

Anne Colby, director of the Murray Research Center, gave us the
opportunity to develop our methodology for presentation in two workshops. We are grateful to Dr. Colby and her splendid staff for these
teaching experiences, and we are hopeful that this monograph will
enhance the Murray Research Center's valiant effort to cultivate more
effective uses of longitudinal data in the study of individual lives. A
great many colleagues helped us to produce a more useful monograph
through their careful reading and feedback, among them Dr. Colby, Tom
Cook, and Jeanne Brooks-Gunn. We are grateful to all and especially
for Robert Merton's incomparable editorial insights. The ultimate test
will come when faculty, practitioners, and students put these methods
to work on their research problems. We invite your recommendations
and suggestions.

—*Glen H. Elder, Jr.*
Eliza K. Pavalko
Elizabeth C. Clipp

WORKING WITH ARCHIVAL DATA
Studying Lives

GLEN H. ELDER, Jr.
University of North Carolina at Chapel Hill

ELIZA K. PAVALKO
Indiana University

ELIZABETH C. CLIPP
Duke University

1. INTRODUCTION

> The originating question must still be recast to indicate the observations that will provide a provisional answer to it. Only then has the problem been definitely posed. (Merton, 1959, p. xxvi)

The growth of longitudinal data archives is one of the most dramatic recent developments in the behavioral sciences. The past 20 years of research depict a sharply rising number of studies in which people are followed across time. The birth of these studies came hard and slow during the 1960s. However, expanding financial resources for research grants made possible the initiation of major nationwide samples by the decade's end. Most notable are the National Longitudinal Surveys, launched during the last years of the 1960s, along with the Michigan Panel Study of Income Dynamics. Countless other longitudinal studies enable access to the original open-ended interviews and observations, as well as to a variety of personal documents (Allport, 1942), from letters and diaries to family records.

Our use of the term *data archives* refers in particular to studies of this kind that Young, Savela, and Phelps (1991) inventoried briefly, such as the well-known longitudinal studies at the Institute of Human Development, University of California, Berkeley. Data on the study members from the late 1920s to the 1980s include observational, interview, and questionnaire information on multiple respondents. When data are based

1

solely on a fixed-response survey (e.g., the National Longitudinal Surveys), they offer very limited possibilities for developing new codes and recasting data sets to fit the questions we pose—a focal point of this monograph. For a description of data resources at the Henry A. Murray Research Center of Radcliffe College, see the appendix.

From calls for greater investment in longitudinal studies across the 1970s and 1980s, we turn to the challenge of the 1990s: making optimal use of these data. How can these data be used in effective ways to study human lives and the life course in a changing society? This question guides our deliberations in this monograph. What an investigator plans to do with archival data necessarily depends on the research problem. At first this problem may be no more than a hunch or vague initiative, an originating question that is little more than a "prelude to the formulation of a problem" (Merton, 1959, p. xix). In some cases originating questions are coupled with a developed rationale about why they are worth asking and pursuing in lieu of other inquiries. Data libraries and funding agencies generally require statements of rationale to enable their selection of the most worthy applicants. But whatever form the question takes, it provides an essential direction in the search for relevant data. However, the task of coming up with a research question is deceptively simple.

> At first appearance, it would seem fairly easy to see and to pose a problem in a branch of science. Surely the raising of questions presents no great difficulty; children do it all the time. And yet, the experience of scientists is summed up in the adage that it is often more difficult to find and to formulate a problem than to solve it. (Merton, 1959, p. ix)

This is so in part because we are referring to a specific kind of question that qualifies as a scientific problem and generates empirical answers that modify, revise, or confirm knowledge in the area, including the originating question itself. Such questions are also subject to modification or refinement as one works with the data. The more one learns about an archive of life-history information, the more one can press a research question toward greater clarity. One may also reshape the data at hand in ways that will make them more responsive to the initial problem. This refinement is achieved through a process of coding or recoding. Here we refer to the interactive dynamic between research question and archival data as a *recasting* process. During a research project, initial questions are reformulated to fit the data and the data are reworked in coding and recoding to fit the question better.

The relative fit between research questions on life-course issues and the availability of life-record data in archives or files has changed dramatically over the past century. Though at present archival files of life-record data typically await probing questions on the life course, in the 1920s such questions far exceeded the longitudinal archives available for pursuing them (most were retrospective or document based). However, inspired by Thomas and Znaniecki's *The Polish Peasant in Europe and America* (1918-1920), researchers in that decade began to use life records to analyze individual lives and human development. The studies undertaken then include the well-known Lewis Terman Study of highly able Californians, a longitudinal study begun in 1922 at Stanford University and still continuing past its twelfth wave of data collection (Minton, 1988a, 1988b), as well as studies at the Institute of Human Development, University of California, Berkeley (Eichorn, Clausen, Haan, Honzik, & Mussen, 1981).

W. I. Thomas, a leading sociologist, clearly expressed the need for prospective studies that follow people over time. He valued qualitative case studies of people over time as well as the quantitative study of lives, and he knew well the pioneering longitudinal projects at Stanford and Berkeley. Moreover, Thomas argued persuasively for the establishment of data archives suited to the temporal questions being asked of lives and human development. In the mid-1920s, Thomas urged giving priority to "the longitudinal approach to life history" (in Volkart, 1951, p. 593). Studies, he observed, should investigate "many types of individuals with regard to their experiences and various past periods of life in different situations" and follow "groups of individuals into the future, getting a continuous record of experiences as they occur." This agenda, so contemporary in many respects, was largely ignored from the 1930s to the 1960s, when the modern survey reigned supreme as a data collection design. All of this changed in the 1960s, as the study of lives and aging became a paramount enterprise.

To appreciate the task of fitting research questions and archival data on lives, we begin with the various strands of the life-course revolution of the 1960s, from theory to statistical techniques, data, and questions. Matching research questions and data is only one important part of this broad development—however, it is arguably the most neglected part. The cupboard is almost completely bare of literature on problem finding and problem formulation, and until recently the use of life-history data from archives was not informed by literature or training. The opportunities data archives offer to potential users have no doubt been encouraging, but all too frequently inquiries and even short-term explorations have not borne fruit. Potential users seldom manage to derive anything of significance for research purposes.

Why is this so? After many years of life-course research with archival data, we believe that the major barrier to effective use of longitudinal files at data libraries has much to do with an undeveloped concept of the relation between research questions and archival data. First, instead of collecting data to address a particular question, the archival investigator searches for data that are well suited to a particular research problem. Knowledge of potential archives represents an essential step in this search, and we briefly survey some of the key archives to highlight issues and considerations in developing an effective use of the data. Second, a thorough inventory of an archive tells what must be done to make the data more responsive to the research problem. Third, reviewing the data also may provide ideas about appropriate modifications in the problem formulation itself. Both types of adjustment— changing the data to fit the question and changing the question to fit the data—tend to occur in a process of relating models or questions to data.

Each of the following chapters provides an application of the model-fitting process to longitudinal data from a single study—the Lewis Terman Study at Stanford University. The original project that led to this perspective and related procedures focused on effects of the Great Depression in the lives of men and women (Elder, 1974). We have continued to refine the approach in longitudinal studies up to the present, currently with the Terman archive of life-record data on men and women born between the early 1900s and 1920. Our initial use of the Terman data dealt with the impact of military service on men's lives, building on more than 20 years of similar work on longitudinal studies housed at the Institute of Human Development, Berkeley.

We have organized this monograph along the lines of workshops we codirected with George and Caroline Vaillant at the Henry Murray Research Center at Radcliffe College in 1989 and 1991. Chapter 2 provides an outline of the general issues and perspectives in working with archival data. Chapter 3 lays out a stepwise account of our approach to the recasting of data to achieve a better fit with research questions on emotional and physical health. Chapter 4 focuses on work life, with emphasis on the later years, and shows how to adapt an existing coding scheme, designed for cross-sectional data, to the temporal patterns characteristic of life records. Any complete life-course study seeks to relate lives to historical change, and in Chapter 5 we outline how we used the Terman data to capture the World War II experiences of the men. All three chapters on applications are based on the Terman men because the archival work we report is part of a longitudinal study of military experiences in men's lives. Our data preparation on the Terman women and their life courses is following the approach employed for the men.

In each recasting effort outlined in the chapters that follow, we were faced with major data limitations in relation to our research questions. Such limitations raise a common dilemma in using archives. How can contemporary questions be illuminated by archival data that were never designed to answer them? While there is no simple answer to this question, the examples in the following chapters should provide some understanding of the decisions and issues involved in the recasting process. We turn now to the relation between data archives and research questions as key elements of the life-course revolution and its paradigm.

2. WORKING WITH ARCHIVAL DATA

In working with archival data, the investigator seeks to maximize the fit between the research question and the data. In one version of this process, life-record data are sought to fit a particular question, then modified or *recast* in some way to achieve a better fit. An improved fit may also be achieved by modifying the research question and its analytical model. In other cases, the question is put aside to enable study of a researchable problem that has relevant data at hand. Most uses of archival data involve a mix of such changes in a sequential process that eventually produces an acceptable goodness of fit.

Variations on this methodology have been applied for many decades by historians and social scientists who use archival data to address their research questions. As a rule, however, these investigators did not develop their procedures in written form as a logic of inquiry or methodology. The pressures of research seldom leave time for self-conscious thought about procedures of this kind. In lieu of formal guidance, research assistants simply learned about the approach through apprenticeships on projects. In this manner, procedures eventually became part of the oral tradition of research on a particular project or in a university institute, passed down across generations of new students.

This informal and idiosyncratic approach to a vital operation in research is no longer sufficient for the task at hand. A revolution in life-course studies and their craft has occurred since the 1960s, and fast-moving developments since then have magnified the need for a systematic account of procedures in working with archival data, with emphasis on the fitting of questions and data.

We begin this chapter by surveying some of these developments in data, theory, and method, as well as their relations to each other and to particular research questions. Advances in one area, such as the dramatic growth of longitudinal data, have implications for related developments in theory and method. Data on sequences of life events call for ways of thinking about them in conceptual terms, and then designing an appropriate statistical analysis. One of the clearest examples of interlocking developments involves the relation between data and the research question. The emergence of new questions about life transitions and aging should prompt fresh thinking about data needs and lead to the establishment of appropriate longitudinal studies. The availability of new longitudinal data sets may encourage investigators to formulate questions that draw on the strengths of such data. Mere exposure to life records that span decades can provide insights on aging that shape the questions of an investigator. We address the interplay between archival data and research questions in the second part of this chapter by describing some older longitudinal data archives.

The revolution in life-course studies and the interplay between longitudinal data archives and research questions bring us to the process of asking new questions of old data. An archive of longitudinal data is necessarily a repository of old data collected in another time and place to investigate questions that earlier investigators posed (Hyman, 1972). The new investigator thus asks new questions of the data set, setting in motion a model-fitting enterprise. Can we address a certain question with the data at hand? If not, can the data be reworked to provide a better fit? Is the recasting effort too costly in time, energy, and funds? And what are its chances of success? We address these questions in the last part of this chapter. Ultimately, we assume that data archives are selected to provide the best fit possible to research questions.

The Life-Course Revolution

The decade of the 1960s gave birth to interrelated developments that have literally transformed the study of lives within the social sciences and history. New theory emerged from the intellectual challenges of increasing longevity and a rapidly changing social world. A longer life span raised questions concerning its quality and the consequences of early experiences for successful aging. Social discontinuities at the time also prompted new questions regarding the connections among lives, generations, and history. Out of this context and scholarship on age came a view of the life course embedded in social institutions and subject to historical forces and cohort influences.

As a concept, the *life course* refers to age-graded life patterns in society (Elder, 1985, 1992). Age differences across the life course take the form of expectations and options that influence plans, choices, and actions, giving shape to life stages, transitions, and turning points. The life course evolves over a relatively long span, as implied by the concept of a trajectory of work, earnings, or marriage, and also over a short time in social transitions—leaving home, entering college, getting and leaving a job.

Transitions are always embedded in trajectories that give them distinctive form and meaning. Thus a particular life trajectory can be charted by linking states across successive years, the states of marriage or employment and earnings. But the meaning of a transition depends on when it occurs in the life course. Loss of employment has one set of meanings and implications when it occurs in the midst of family formation and quite another after the children have left home. Likewise, loss of a spouse is expectable after age 65 or 70, but not in early adulthood, where it has more profound and enduring effects on the surviving mate's mental state (McLanahan & Sorensen, 1985).

A number of conceptual distinctions mark off contemporary views of life-course theory from such perspectives in the 1950s. First and most important, lives and society are now recognized as interlocking processes. Life patterns are shaped by institutional, cultural, and material changes occurring in society; these changes occur in part through changes in people. Birth cohorts age in different ways in a changing society (Riley, Johnson, & Foner, 1972; Ryder, 1965). Second, attention to historical variation is coupled with a contemporary appreciation of variable age patterns over the life course. Contrary to modal notions about age and life events in cultures—that people of the same age march in concert across major life events—the contemporary perspective assumes that life events vary in *timing* and *sequencing,* with real consequences for people and society (Hogan, 1981). A third distinct feature of contemporary views on the life course underscores the *interdependence* of life transitions and experiences over the life span. Variations in the social timing of marriage, children, and residential change may be expressed in choices made later in life.

From the 1960s to the present, developing theory on the life course has defined a context for empirical inquiry, including relevant problems and variables, and structured the generation of evidence and hypotheses. As a theoretical orientation, the life-course framework suggests research questions, rationales for why they are worthy of study, and actual lines of analysis. The influence process also works the other way, from new research needs and questions to the enhanced appeal of the life-course framework.

Two other developments in the 1960s had consequences for an emerging framework of life-course study and helped to shape a life-course paradigm: the growth of longitudinal data plus the discovery of archival materials, and the development of new statistical analysis and data collection techniques (Bollen, 1989; Mayer & Tuma, 1990; Tuma & Hannan, 1984). These interdependencies can be pictured as a triangle with points representing data, method, and theory. Innovations at any point in the system have consequences for all other points. The spread of event history statistical models has shaped theories of aging (Featherman & Lerner, 1985) as well as data requirements.

For reasons only vaguely understood, the decade of the 1960s witnessed an unparalleled expansion of prospective longitudinal studies, from the huge Project Talent sample to the nationwide Panel Study of Income Dynamics at the University of Michigan and the National Longitudinal Surveys, along with countless small projects (Brooks-Gunn, Phelps, & Elder, 1991). These initiatives spurred the development and application of techniques suited to the analysis of event sequences and histories in dynamic models and the assessment of causal paths across the life span (Campbell & O'Rand, 1988). In turn, the data requirements of specific techniques established standards for collecting life-record data, such as the need for continuous record information in event history analysis.

Michigan's Panel Study of Income Dynamics (Duncan & Morgan, 1985) illustrates some of these interconnections. This data archive is a product of one of the most ambitious panel studies ever launched in the United States. Established at the end of the War on Poverty to address issues of welfare dependency and persistent poverty, the Michigan Panel of more than 6,000 families nationwide has generated data each year from 1968 to the present. Some 20,000 people are involved. The study was not designed initially for research into the life course, but perspectives on the life course have marked the data in at least three respects. First, more users of the data are developing longitudinal analyses—in the past, cross-sectional uses were surprisingly common. Second, questions have been added over the years to complete event histories and enrich the body of life-record information on people and families. Third, study of individual family members emerged as the most effective way to study the family, because individuals remain unique over time, while family situations change constantly. Studying the careers and relationships of individuals in the Michigan Panel clearly favors a concept of family patterns as an evolving family life course.

Longitudinal studies begun in the 1960s were especially instrumental in developing notions about the life course through the empirical facts and questions about lives they produced. One example of this point comes from the Michigan Panel and centers on prevailing beliefs about poverty, such as that it is self-perpetuating: People enter poverty through misfortune or the inheritance of values and seldom manage to become self-supporting again. Contrary to such beliefs at the time, the Michigan Panel found that only a very small proportion of sample members who actually experienced poverty did so beyond a year (Duncan, 1984). Transient members of the poverty group turned out to be indistinguishable from members of the general sample, while chronic cases were typically in one or more of three categories—black, old, or female. Empirical findings of this kind focused attention on whether and how disadvantaged people managed to surmount their limitations. What pathways did they follow to the adult years?

The life-course revolution, with its dramatic change in how we think about and study the human life course, represents one part of a general paradigm change that has made time, context, and process more salient dimensions of theory and analysis in the social sciences. Theoretical ideas on the life course were coupled with appropriate data resources and methodology for the investigation of aging and the effects of social change. Since then, advances in life-course theory, longitudinal studies, and statistical analysis have been covered periodically by workshops, manuals, and books.

Neglected in all of this is the process by which longitudinal data are fitted to research questions and theory. This process applies to contemporary archives of longitudinal data as well as to older ones. The challenge is greater with the older archives because the technology of data collection has changed so much over the years, along with our theories and methods. We turn now to some of these older data archives and to the task they present for the user with specific research questions.

Asking New Questions of Old Data

The early era of life study in the United States was distinguished by a surge of life-span questions that far exceeded the available longitudinal data for addressing them. Nevertheless, path-breaking efforts were underway during the 1930s to follow individuals into their future with periodic data collection. These include the Lewis Terman Study at Stanford University (birth years 1904-1920; see Minton, 1988a, 1988b) and three longitudinal projects launched across San Francisco Bay at the Institute of Child Welfare (now called Human Development) at the University of California, Berkeley: the Berkeley Growth Study, the Berkeley Guidance Study (both with birth years of 1928-1929), and the Oakland Growth Study (birth years 1920-1921) (Eichorn et al., 1981).

None of these California studies was initially conceived as following children into the later years of life, yet each has done so up to the 1980s—a truly remarkable feat under difficult circumstances. Nancy Bayley directed the Berkeley Growth Study for many years until her retirement; Jean MacFarlane established and directed the Berkeley Guidance Study across her professional life; and Harold and Mary Jones were primary figures in directing the Oakland Growth Study (Jones, Bayley, MacFarlane, & Honzik, 1971). Lewis Terman (1925) directed his study of gifted Californians until he died in 1956.

Our common attraction to these data archives centered around the influence of historical change on the lives of men and women from different birth cohorts. Children in the Oakland and Berkeley cohorts grew up during the Great Depression and experienced the mobilization of World War II, but neither of these historical changes was considered relevant to developmental issues at the time. The larger historical world of the investigators and study members did not inform the conceptual models of the projects.

Nevertheless, the investigators collected some information on the larger environment that years later provided the basis for empirical studies of depression hardship and wartime experience in lives (Elder, 1974, 1979, 1986, 1987). Empirical findings from studies of the Second World War in lives posed questions that called for analysis in another sample of American men who served during this war. We chose to work on the Terman sample because of its rich data on World War II veterans.

A neglect of historical facts also appears in the Terman Study and its priorities on data collection. A large number of the men finished school and started careers during the Great Depression, and nearly half entered the military during World War II. Depression and war virtually defined their collective life for 12 successive years, yet the Terman Study almost failed to collect any information on life experience through the 1930s and World War II. The 1950 follow-up was equally silent on World War II, much to the disbelief of some of the men who served (45% of the sample). Despite the neglect of history in the study records, the archive of letters and notes permitted some exploration of historical times in the lives of this extraordinary sample of men and women.

In our work with these archival data, the following lessons and themes emerged:

1. Archival data are never precisely what one wants or expects. Given this, the investigator is challenged to do what is possible, given time and resources, in shaping the data according to needs. These operations are included under Herbert Hyman's (1972) philosophy for secondary analysts, that of "making the best of what one has."

2. The data at hand reflect the perspectives of the original investigators, as expressed in research questions, data collection procedures, and analytic techniques. These perspectives also reflect the scientific and cultural themes of the historical era (see Minton, 1988a, 1988b).

3. Longitudinal data archives do not guarantee life-record or longitudinal data analysis. Cross-sectional data entries and storage are far more common than temporal records of information on people's lives, and often these cross-sectional records have to be converted to a life-record format.

4. Life-course studies can draw on quantitative and qualitative data and analyses. Effective use of both kinds of data requires careful planning to permit their application to identical topics or problems.

5. The rationale for using archival data should be based on strengths of the data. It should not be defended through attempts to disarm or ignore the weaknesses.

An example of the fourth lesson at work comes from John Laub and Robert Sampson, who have resurrected an old data archive on delinquent males created by Eleanor and Sheldon Glueck in the 1930s. Noting that they were often questioned about the contemporary relevance of the "old data," Laub (1991) reports that they decided to emphasize how the data represent strategic research materials:

> Because these data are "old" they provide an unusual opportunity to assess whether the causes of both juvenile delinquency and adult crime are specific to a historical period. The data can also be used to assess changes in the system response to crime. (p. 7)

The five points above have illustrations in the Terman and Berkeley studies. As the oldest ongoing longitudinal study, the Terman Study is our point of departure.

THE TERMAN STUDY

During the waning of the eugenics movement and its hereditarian interests, psychologist Lewis Terman launched a study in 1921-1922 to investigate the maintenance of early intellectual superiority over a 10-year period. This objective was soon extended into the adult years for the purpose of determining the life paths of these gifted Californians. Terman believed that, by identifying the most gifted at a young age, society could ensure the flow of talent to leadership positions.

Aided by his assistants, Terman selected, from large and medium-sized urban areas of California, 857 boys and 671 girls ages 3 to 19 years who had IQs above 135 (Minton, 1988a, 1988b; Terman & Oden, 1959). So far, 13 waves of data collection have been carried out, beginning in 1921-1922 with interviews of parents and the study children and an array of tests and inventories (Table 2.1).

The first 1922 and 1928 data collections focused on family life and school experience, and included interviews and questionnaires involving mothers of children in the study. Fathers were not thought to be important in child rearing, at least compared with mothers, so they were excluded from data collection. The 1936 and 1940 follow-ups occurred at a time of educational achievement and the start of adult careers for many, whether marriage, family, or work. At the next follow-up, questions were asked about these topics, the war, and various service roles. The postwar years through 1960 were times of marriage and family development, career beginnings, and accomplishment. Each topic was investigated by mail (1950, 1955, 1960). Various life changes within the Terman sample and new leadership from Robert Sears, Lee Cronbach, Pauline Sears, and Albert Hastorf brought fresh attention to issues of aging, work life and retirement, family, and life evaluation across follow-ups for 1972, 1977, 1982, 1986, and 1991-1992.

Data collection across multiple waves relies mainly on survey forms mailed to the study members. The slender base of financial support for the study and the large sample size favored this least expensive method. However, the files include a rich selection of other data, such as news clippings, interviews with parents, questionnaires from spouses, letters from study members, other record data, and birth and death certificates.

TABLE 2.1
Terman Longitudinal Sample and Data

Survey Waves	Number of Respondents	Primary Topics
1922 1928	1,528: 857 men, 671 women	home and school
1936 1940	1,256: 699 men, 557 women	education, work, marriage
1945	1,334: 749 men, 585 women	military experience
1950	1,271: 716 men, 555 women	
1955	1,286: 716 men, 570 women	work, marriage, achievements
1960	1,127: 616 men, 511 women	
1972	927: 497 men, 430 women	
1977	812: 426 men, 386 women	aging, work and retirement,
1982	813: 415 men, 398 women	life review
1986	805: 404 men, 401 women	
1991-1992	follow-up in progress	

The letters, in particular, add a great deal of richness beyond the often narrow structure of the survey forms.

Men shared work and military experiences with Terman, frequently in requests for letters of recommendation to prospective employers or for advice on personal matters. Women stressed the lives of their children in letters to the Terman Study office. The wealth of these materials in the study files provides an option for the user who is not satisfied with the data on file. A researcher can always develop new codes and apply them to the qualitative material.

The full value of any longitudinal study comes from life records that draw on all waves of data, such as the 13 points of data collection on the Terman sample. Life records enable the investigator to follow people across events that mark changes in work and family life. However, the machine-readable Terman data were stored by each wave at the Inter-University Consortium for Political and Social Research, with each data wave functioning as a cross-sectional entry instead of as part of a life history or record. Cross-sectional entries of this kind favor studies that merely correlate states or processes at different stages of life, as distinct from research that delineates life trajectories. With our life-course objectives in mind, one of our first tasks entailed preparation of life records on work, earnings, marriage, parenthood, and health from the computerized data. We supplemented this work with a series of new codes on the life course and historical experience, a task requiring a number of weeks of archival research at the Stanford research center.

With origins mainly in the upper middle class, the Terman men and women generally experienced strong encouragement and financial support for higher education. A majority completed four years of college, and a similar proportion pursued advanced studies and degrees. More than 90% eventually married, and approximately 85% of the marriages survived to old age. Four-fifths were located in the upper middle class during the 1960s. This class bias and the bias on measured intelligence define narrow boundaries for generalization, though both can be seen as the strength of a study that explores the life-course effects of social change. Men and women from this stratum would be especially sensitive to the impact of historical change in their lives.

At the very outset of work with the Terman data, we thought we could rely on the available files of coded information. After much exploration, described in Chapters 3 through 5, we found that we could not address our questions with the machine-readable data in their present form. The data were not what we wanted, and thus we launched a major effort to recast them through new codes. We did not easily choose this course of action, and the reason can be best understood in terms of prior work with longitudinal data at the Institute of Human Development, University of California, Berkeley.

FROM OLD DATA TO NEW QUESTIONS: CHILDREN OF THE GREAT DEPRESSION

We came to the Terman Study in the mid-1980s after many years of research with longitudinal data from the Oakland Growth Study archive and, later, from the Berkeley Growth and Guidance Studies (Elder, 1992). As might be expected, these data played a different role in our work from those of the Terman data, especially in their initial stage.

The materials helped to shape a research perspective on social change in lives and to crystallize a suitable way of thinking about questions of this kind and their empirical study—now frequently described as a *life-course perspective.* Over time, both research questions and the perspective helped to specify data requirements and the need for new codes, as they did in the Terman Study. As a result of this background, we came to its data with a relatively clear sense of problem and a developed research plan.

The senior author began work with the longitudinal data of the Oakland Growth Study in 1962, during his tenure at the University of California, Berkeley, and its Institute of Human Development. The Oakland Growth Study began in 1931 under the pioneering leadership of Harold E. Jones and Herbert R. Stolz, then research director and director, respectively, of the Institute of Child Welfare. Fifth- and sixth-grade children were selected for the study from elementary schools in northeastern Oakland, California (Eichorn et al., 1981). The study aimed to investigate normal development—biological, psychological, and social. Data were collected annually from teachers, study participants, peers, and staff observers. Mothers were interviewed in 1932, 1934, and 1936. Annual data collections were carried out across the 1930s, followed by five waves of data collection in the adult years, 1953, 1958-1960, 1964, 1970-1972, and 1981-1982. The follow-ups generally included interviews, health assessments, personality inventories, and fact-sheet questionnaires.

By the early 1960s the Oakland Study had just entered its third decade, with study members at mid-life. More than 200 data sets were available for computer analysis, but the data could not provide an event history on study members' lives. For example, we could not determine how many of the boys had served in World War II and what proportion had been called back into active duty during the Korean conflict. Nothing was available on the women's work histories and their wartime experiences. The life courses of the study members had not been charted. One reason for this deficiency involved the way the archival data had been stored.

All of the machine-readable data were organized according to age and/or grade by particular inventory. And most analyses up to that point had merely correlated items from inventories at different points in time. The intervening years remained a mystery in the absence of coded life histories. No data set had information on the socioeconomic histories of study members or on the timetables of events in their adult lives. Marital and parental histories were fragmentary. In view of this situation, constructing life histories became a priority task on the project, calling for fresh thinking about process, time, and context.

Contrary to static notions about social class and family life, the Oakland Growth Study archives depicted families in almost constant change. From day to day, the economic circumstances of families were subject to change—family members entered and left the labor force, households expanded through births and visitors, and family consumption changed to meet available income and member needs. This moving picture of family change prompted serious thinking about how family adaptations to income loss construct a life course (Elder, 1974). For example, one set of adaptations entailed a shift in the family economy from capital- to labor-intensive activity. Goods and services were produced by the labor of family members. Children and mothers assumed a more central role in the productive activities of hard-pressed families.

Changes in the family provided a way of relating the Oakland children to the generalized economic decline and fluctuations of the 1930s. Some Oakland families lost heavily and others fared well; indeed, some even prospered because their losses did not match the decline in cost of living (about 25% by 1933). Using family income data in 1929 and 1933, we decided to classify families with a loss of more than 34% as economically deprived. The data were not adequate to array families as a continuum on percentage loss or change (subjective measures of hardship were also included in the study). All other families became nondeprived. The basic design compared nondeprived and deprived families within the middle and working classes as of 1929. Class position in 1929 thus defined a cultural and economic context in which families worked out lines of adaptation to deprivation, including changes in the family economy, altered family relations, and the management of social strains within the family.

A second part of the task centered on ways of thinking about the lives of individuals. How are lives socially patterned, and what does this phrase actually mean? The concept of career offered ideas about single paths mainly in the field of work, but lives combined multiple paths and their interconnections over time. More useful at the time were the social meanings of age in expectations, stages and categories, and sanctions. As a whole, the social meanings of age and kinship status provide a perspective on the social patterning of life events and activities. In particular, we refer to the social timing of events, such as marriage and work, and the age-graded structure of life trajectories. Efforts to use the Oakland data archive to study lives proved to be a developmental experience in life-course thinking. This new learning was soon expressed in coding forms that brought process, time, and context to an empirical representation of the Oakland life course in a changing world.

Three phases were identified conceptually for coding purposes—preadult, young adult, and the later years. The preadult phase focused exclusively on the social and economic careers of families. In adulthood, the initial phase of young adulthood centered on the transition markers to adulthood (the time when particular events occurred and the like) and on the establishment years of family formation and work-life development. The later phase began after age 35-40 and was structured primarily by work and family patterns. One of the most important conceptual influences on this coding operation came from Harold Wilensky's (1961) Labor and Leisure Study in Detroit. Wilensky's project addressed the interplay of three life lines—labor, leisure, and family. A review of his codebook spurred our thinking about concepts of life transition, interdependence, and trajectories.

The three years of preparatory work for a study of children of the Great Depression broke new ground for us, because we could not fall back on tried-and-true approaches. The archival work represented an apprenticeship in the design of a life-history study, especially in producing a match between life-course questions and data. By the time we had decided to develop a comparative cohort study with longitudinal data from the Berkeley Guidance Study (early 1970s), the methodology of doing such archival work was reasonably clear.

The Berkeley Guidance Study archive itself was larger than that of the Oakland Study because more generations were included. In Figure 2.1, Box 1 refers solely to the Oakland Study and includes two generations, with most of the data on subjects born between 1920 and 1921. The project in Box 2 involves a comparison of the Oakland and Berkeley cohorts on the depression experience (Elder, 1979). Data were also collected on Berkeley parents from young adulthood to old age, and on the study children, their postwar children, and grandparents. The project in Box 3 focuses on the intergenerational dynamics that link the generations (Elder, Caspi, & Downey, 1986), as in the reproduction of parental behavior styles.

From the original sample of Guidance Study members, 214 were followed through the 1930s and early 1940s; 182 were members of the study through age 40 or 1970. Data on their origins and early life courses to 1930 were obtained from the parents in 1929-1930. Annual data (1929-1945) on parents, children, and the family as a whole came from observations by institute fieldworkers and teachers, and from self-reports (interviews, questionnaires). Postwar data from parents were collected in 1969 and 1973, and from their children—the Berkeley Study members—in 1960, 1970-1972, and the 1980s.

With the basic features of archival work in mind, we managed to complete all of the life-course coding for the Berkeley study within a year, 1972-1973. This approach anticipated our work with the Terman data archive, as presented in this monograph, and consequently provides a useful background on fitting research questions to data.

18

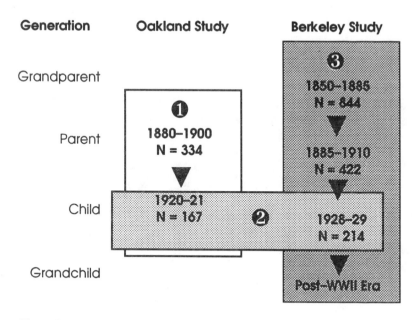

Figure 2.1. Two Intergenerational Studies

FROM LIFE RECORDS TO CODES:
THE BERKELEY GUIDANCE ARCHIVE

Our work in the Guidance Study archive was structured by a comparative objective: a cohort comparison of the effects of depression hardship through the family and into the lives of men and women. From the vantage point of an observer, the archive seemed well matched for such analysis, although the extent of the match and the coding requirements could be determined only through an on-site inventory of the coded and uncoded data. Interviews, home observations, and letters provided many of the uncoded data.

The inventory established a map of the archival territory in relation to objectives and thus enabled more effective use of resources. We needed to know what materials relevant to our questions were still uncoded, what data were coded but not prepared for analysis, and what coded data were acceptable for our purposes. In the course of completing the inventory, we achieved a closer fit between research questions and the Berkeley data as potential and fact. For example, we learned that we could measure depression income loss so that the index would closely match the Oakland measure on change from 1929 to 1933 and also provide a more detailed index of percentage change of total family income.

After several months of intensive work, we had a firm mastery of the lines of inquiry that could be pursued, with and without new codings. As in the Oakland data archive, the inventory produced very few social data that were coded and structured in life-record form. We could readily determine the status of individuals and families at points in time, but we could not ascertain the course they followed over time. Social life histories were not available.

These examples provide some indication of the work required before any coding and recasting of the data archive could begin. Most important, we had to assemble the social data in chronological form to construct life records that would then become the basic data for coding.

A *life record* is a chronology of major life events and experiences, and traditionally there are at least three ways to build one. A life record can be prepared by the respondent from a personal perspective, as in oral histories (Hareven, 1982). Life records on a particular person are also produced from the perspective of an informant or knowledgeable other, such as a spouse, confidant, or best friend. Finally, life records are sometimes constructed by a third party, such as a clinician or researcher, using a wide array of materials, from written and oral reports by the subject to letters, vital records, observational materials, and public documents from social agencies.

By synthesizing diverse material into a single chronology, the third approach represents an effort to obtain the most complete record in relation to the facts at hand. Disparate reports are resolved with the objective of achieving the most accurate account. For a number of reasons, the Guidance Study archive proved to be ideally suited to the third synthetic approach to life records. The intensively studied families and children were contacted many times each year by a fieldworker, whose field notes became part of the data archive. Other data sources included reports by mothers and the children, teacher ratings and reports, and letters from various agencies.

Thoroughly trained project assistants were instructed to read the case assembly of each family, and then construct life records systematically in eight specialized areas: socioeconomic career of father and family, 1929-1945; work life of male household head; work life of wife and mother; 1929-1945 household composition; parental marital relations,

1929-1945; parent-child relations, 1929-1945, 1969; parents' subjective interpretations of the life course, 1929-1945; and adult life course of study members, 1945-1970s.

The life records were developed to provide codable, longitudinal information on the family unit, mothers and fathers, and study members. The assembled biographical record also offered an empirical base for qualitative case studies. This record was clearly a by-product of the need for life-record data in the coding operation, but it offers so many advantages to the analyst who needs to move back and forth between quantitative data and chronological records that it deserves to be an objective in its own right. Among several computer programs for coding life-history data are TAP, Qualpro, and the Ethnographer (Tesch, 1990).

Life-course analysts encounter many archival challenges, but few are more demanding than the redesign of data sets or a study archive to obtain a better fit between research question and data, a task that becomes more common as we move back in historical time. Data sets that seem appropriate frequently need more investment in measurements and file design than was originally anticipated. In other cases, a longitudinal data archive may represent the last hope among generally undesirable choices for investigating a specific life-history question.

The Oakland Growth and Berkeley Guidance archives posed a challenge because neither represented a complete life-course framework when first encountered. Moreover, neither study was equipped with measures of historical change and experience. Nevertheless, both studies held the potential for life records and quantitative data on lives as well as changing times. Understandably, this potential is much easier to see now than at the beginning, but perhaps this lack of foresight is adaptive. Would a researcher embark on a study requiring such investments if he or she knew the whole story at the outset? Probably not. In this sense, limited vision has unquestioned benefits for long-range accomplishments that can require years of archival work.

Fitting Research Questions and Data

One distinctive feature of the life-course revolution is the birth of numerous longitudinal studies and efforts to follow people who were studied many years ago. Some follow-ups have used life calendars or age-event matrices (Freedman, Thornton, Camburn, Alwin, & Young-DeMarco, 1988) that record the years and months at which events or transitions occur in each activity domain. The cross-check possibilities in such calendars help to minimize errors of recall. These prospective studies and retrospective projects are generating data archives for current investigators and for those who will need life-history data in the future.

Investigators seek to maximize the fit between their research questions and the best available data at hand, but there is generally some disparity between questions and data over the long term. As we have noted, the process of working with archival data typically involves adjustments in questions and data. The interplay is reciprocal. We reformulate questions in light of the data at hand and frequently recast data for a better fit with our questions.

Some of the work of this matching process is achieved in selecting an appropriate data set. We select certain data sets because they presumably enable us to address certain questions. From this angle, the research enterprise is question driven: The question comes first and structures the process. When archival data are available, the investigator occupies the very special position of planning a research program around a central problem. This option is not always available to investigators who are running their own longitudinal studies. Their challenge is to devise research questions that can be addressed by the data archive. In this sense, data shape the agenda by defining what is and is not possible.

In our review of the Terman, Oakland, and Berkeley data archives, we have mentioned a series of steps in the process of working with archival data and of seeking to achieve an optimum fit between research questions and data (see Figure 2.2). The Terman Study very nicely illustrates the steps. We begin with *problem specification* and the premise that it is valuable to have a well-honed sense of the problem before beginning the *search for an appropriate data set or archive*. The Terman Study met our needs because nearly half of the men served in World War II, and at relatively late ages. The Oakland and Berkeley studies had told us that relatively late mobilization was most depriving for military personnel. The Terman data archive, then, provided an opportunity to explore the very worst match between men and service entry, a transition time that increased the risk of divorce and career disruption. In our search for appropriate data, we were unable to find a better resource for our purposes.

With the options surveyed, the stage is set for *preparing a research proposal* that makes the very best case for the goodness of fit between data and question. As noted earlier, the most effective strategy is to make a case for the advantages of the data. Almost by definition,

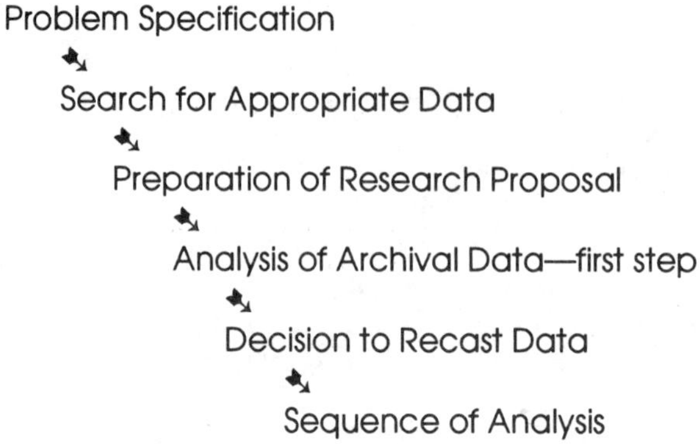

Problem Specification

Search for Appropriate Data

Preparation of Research Proposal

Analysis of Archival Data—first step

Decision to Recast Data

Sequence of Analysis

Figure 2.2. Steps in the Research Process

archival data from another era will have numerous limitations when compared with contemporary data and measurements. However, contemporary data will not enable an investigation of issues that extend back in historical time.

Initial analysis of the data may be carried out in preparation for a research proposal, along with a thorough inventory of the coded data. This overview can provide evidence on why *a recasting effort* must be made, and it might indicate the need to seek other data. Our plans to develop a battery of new codes from the Terman data files were made only when we realized that we had no alternative if we expected to carry out a satisfying study.

As the subsequent chapters make clear, we put off recasting as long as possible because we knew the amount of work it entailed. Our deepening awareness of the need for a large recoding effort became persuasive only as we moved well into the stage of *data analysis.* By comparison, the need for new codes and recasting in the Oakland and Berkeley studies was clear at the outset, and we encountered few surprises in the course of completing this work.

Conclusion

The central theme of this chapter brings to mind an earlier time in the sociology of science—the 1950s—and a series of thoughtful essays by

Robert K. Merton (1959, 1968) on the contributions of empirical research to theory, the relation between sociological theory and research, and the task of problem finding. The essays were written well before the 1960s and the life-course revolution, but none since has proved more helpful in understanding this change in thinking and research, particularly its systemic nature. Breakthroughs were achieved in theory, methods, data, and research questions, and all of these developments are interrelated. The remarkable expansion of longitudinal databases challenges theory and statistical models, and the development of new "quantitative methods permits new conceptualizations" (Campbell & O'Rand, 1988, p. 66).

The neglected link in this system of change is the relation between data and research question—the central domain of this chapter, as we have seen, and as we shall see, of the following ones as well. Archival work that leads to empirical research involves a process of maximizing the fit between data and research questions. The enterprise includes two interactive operations: reformulating questions and models to provide a better fit with given data and recasting data to provide a better fit with questions and analytic models. Typically these adjustments occur concurrently. The working process yields, ideally, a clearer sense of problem, a more detailed statement of the analytic model, and suitable life-record codes. Although recasting data archives occurs in part through the coding process, no research activity is more conceptual in nature.

3. RECASTING THE ARCHIVE

An investigator whose research question cannot be answered satisfactorily through the use of existing data has several options. One is to give up the project entirely and turn to other matters, but this solution is scarcely optimal. Alternatively, the question can be reformulated to achieve a better fit, or the archive can be recast to address the question more adequately. It is also possible to make both adjustments. As a guide for the researcher who decides to recast a data archive, we focus on the recasting process and provide essential details concerning the practical operations in each stage.

The decision to recast a data archive should not be taken lightly, for it can involve a major outlay of intellectual and material resources over an extended period of time. By *recasting,* we have in mind more than simply a recoding exercise. Recasting may entail some recoding, but

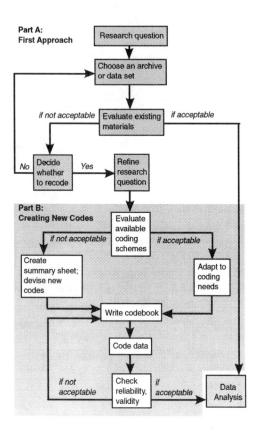

Figure 3.1. Recasting the Archive: The Decision Process

the most fundamental operation entails a new theoretical model and efforts to shape the data for a satisfactory empirical test.

The data in this case are not recoded; they are restructured to provide completely new measures of the concepts (see Figure 3.1). To illustrate, we divide the steps into two approaches, evaluation and recasting. The first approach (gray boxes) represents an archive evaluation phase; the second (white boxes) depicts the recasting phase.

The first approach entails choosing and evaluating an archive. Investigators have rarely had to recode secondary data in recent years because study designs, both cross-sectional and longitudinal, have been sophisticated, eclectic, and adaptable to a variety of research questions and methods. Furthermore, data collection instruments in contemporary studies are often too highly structured to enable the substantial recasting of measures. However, some research questions, particularly those that deal with social and historical change, can be answered only with older archival materials. These archives were never intended to address the questions that interest investigators today; consequently, contemporary approaches often involve reworking the archives. Luckily, original questionnaires and other data sources are usually accessible in older archives, providing an option of recoding not available in contemporary data sets.

For these reasons, anyone using archival data must carefully evaluate the quality of the existing codes and the potential costs and benefits of recoding. If the existing codes are adequate, data analysis can begin, but if they are not, the researcher must decide whether to recast the archive or look for an alternate data source.

The second stage of the recasting process begins once a decision has been made to rework the data and refine the research questions. The first steps in creating new codes are to evaluate other coding schemes carefully to determine whether those measures can be adapted to these data or whether the researcher must develop entirely new codes. If standardized codes can be used, the researcher must go through a process of adapting them to the data.

However, if the research questions or the form of the data make other schemes inapplicable, we recommend developing a summary sheet to inventory each case and to aid in the development of new codes. Further details regarding creation and use of summary sheets are discussed under Step 4 below. After these preliminary steps are complete, the new variables and codes are documented by the codebook. Next, the cases are coded, and finally, the reliability and validity of the new codes can be estimated. If the data are acceptable, preparations can be made for data analysis. If the reliability or validity is unacceptable, the researcher must return to the codebook, refine the codes, and proceed through the coding operations a second time.

In this chapter, we illustrate the process by detailing our construction of new health codes on data collected between 1945 and 1986 for men in the Terman archive. Creating health codes for the Terman men is an especially good example of how to capitalize on the full potential of an archive. The study was never designed to examine health, but even the minimal collection of self-reported health and illnesses at each survey wave allows us to reconceptualize health as a temporal process that unfolds across the life span. Our temporal conceptualization of health is uniquely designed for these data, but the stages of evaluation, reformulation, operationalization, and reevaluation are not—they are basic stages in the recasting of any data archive.

First Approach

STEP 1: EVALUATION OF EXISTING MATERIALS

Any use of an archive should be guided by a researchable question that enables the investigator to decide whether the data are adequate or, if not, whether recoding is necessary and possible. Our interest in health was framed within a larger research agenda focused on military service and adult development. We were particularly interested in learning how military experience affected emotional and physical health immediately after an individual's return to civilian life, as well as how such experience influenced long-term patterns of health and aging. The Terman archive was promising for answering such questions because it included a supplemental questionnaire in 1945, and several health questions were repeated in all survey waves.

Another advantage of the Terman archive is that all survey data have been coded, entered, and documented, and are available on computer tape from the Inter-University Consortium for Political and Social Research at Ann Arbor. We approached the Terman archive by assuming that we could use the precoded data. As with any secondary data analysis, our initial step was to assemble all precoded health information from 1945 to 1986 (Table 3.1).

After reviewing the health data, we were encouraged by the repetition of three self-reported items: (a) general health since the previous survey wave; (b) illnesses, accidents, or surgery in recent years; and (c) tendencies toward emotional disturbances and worries—including dates and nature of the difficulty and how it was handled (therapy, hospitalization). These questions are available in all eight survey waves from 1945 to 1986. In addition, although the data were coded as cross sections, retrospective questions on health since the prior survey wave tended to fill in the intervals between waves, generating health histories for each respondent.

We knew that minor manipulations of the data would be necessary to adapt the archive to our needs, but the precoded data on computer tape seemed to provide adequate information to answer the research questions

TABLE 3.1
Health Information in Terman Files, 1945-1986

Survey	Age	Variable
1945	35	general physical condition since 1940; illnesses, surgery, accidents in recent years; tendencies toward emotional distress
1950	40	general physical condition since 1945; illnesses, surgery, accidents in recent years; tendencies toward emotional distress; alcohol use—if problem, how handled
1955	45	general physical health since 1950; illnesses, surgery, accidents in recent years; tendencies toward emotional distress
1960	50	general physical health since 1955; illnesses, surgery, accidents in recent years; tendencies toward emotional distress; alcohol use—if problem, how handled
1972	62	general health 1970-1972; major changes in physical or mental well-being; energy and vitality
1977	67	general health 1977; major changes in physical or mental well-being; health compared with peers; energy and vitality; happiness
1982	72	general health since 1976; major changes in physical or mental well-being; aspects of health causing worry; tendencies toward emotional problems; extent of personal care or assistance needed; energy and vitality; mood in last 2 months; happiness
1986	76	general health since 1981; major changes in physical or mental well-being; aspects of health causing worry; extent of personal care or assistance needed; mood in last 2 months; alcohol use—if problem, steps taken; energy and vitality; happiness; bothersome declines in health
Overall		date and rough determination of cause of death

at hand. Not until much later did we realize that the original codes were wholly inadequate and not salvageable. This awareness forced us to reevaluate the materials and eventually to decide on a thorough recasting of the archive. We provide details on this setback to demonstrate the possibilities and limitations of working with preexisting codes.

To adapt the original codes to meet our needs, we began with the most promising indicator of physical health. In all eight survey waves from 1945 to 1986, the men listed their illnesses, surgery, or major changes in mental or physical well-being. The end result is an array of 98 medical conditions (see Table 3.2). Some are well-known conditions, such as diabetes and Parkinson's disease, and some are common surgical procedures, such as gall bladder or prostate surgery; however, other

TABLE 3.2

Examples of Health Conditions Terman Men Listed Across Seven
Waves (1945-1986)

memory loss	lonely, less happy
decreased vigor, fatigue	abscess, cellulitis
hepatitis	pernicious anemia
diabetes	hip fracture
hypertension	hip replacement
myocardial infarction	congestive heart failure
atherosclerosis	stroke
coronary bypass	angina
heart arrhythmia	anxiety, nervousness
depression	gout
multiple sclerosis	migraine headaches
alcoholism	Parkinson's disease
encephalitis	lung cancer
colon cancer	abdominal cancer
skin cancer	leukemia
detached retina	prostate cancer
prostate surgery	kidney stones
mugging with concussion	gall bladder surgery
diverticulosis	hemorrhoids
peptic ulcer	hemorrhoidectomy
appendicitis	cirrhosis of liver
tuberculosis	asthma
emphysema	pneumonia
pulmonary embolism	hearing loss

codes were more obscure in their exact meaning, such as "slowing down," "fatigue," or "lonely."

Our research interests were not focused on the diagnoses or conditions, but on their impact on daily functioning. Thus we needed some way to translate the physical conditions into a measure of impairment and compare levels of impairment across surveys. We adopted the Cumulative Illness Rating Scale (Linn, Linn, & Gurel, 1968) to rate the severity of role impairment for each diagnosis or condition as follows:

0 = *None:* No impairment.

1 = *Mild:* Impairment does not interfere with normal role function; treatment may or may not be required; prognosis is excellent.

2 = *Moderate:* Impairment interferes with normal activity; treatment is needed; prognosis is good.

3 = *Severe:* Impairment is disabling; treatment is urgently needed; prognosis is guarded.

4 = *Extremely Severe:* Impairment is life threatening; treatment is emergent or possibly of no avail; prognosis is grave.

We asked four medical experts to use this scale independently to make clinical judgments on each of the 98 medical conditions. We asked the judges to consider, for example, the degree to which an individual's family and work roles were probably compromised in the presence of a stroke or fractured leg. To determine the approximate degree of impairment the respondent experienced when the condition was first mentioned, we asked the raters to "indicate the code that best describes the degree of impairment in role function experienced by individuals with this problem at the time of diagnosis—please use your judgment in relation to all patients you have observed, on average."

Two of the four raters were physicians, board certified in internal medicine. The other two raters were nurses with advanced degrees—a doctoral candidate in public health and a Ph.D. psychologist. Each rater had at least five years of clinical experience. This medical expertise was confirmed when agreement among all four raters across health conditions exceeded 80%. We were pleased with what promised to be quality impairment data and proceeded to the analysis phase, only to discover major problems in short order.

We first checked the validity of our measures by examining some basic correlates of health, such as age and education, at successive cross sections. According to the research literature, education should have a modest but significant relationship to health, with age becoming more predictive of health over time. To our surprise and puzzlement, these simple expectations received no support. The effects of age and education varied dramatically from one measurement to the next, with no logical pattern. In one survey wave, age and education were highly significant predictors of health. The relationship disappeared in the next wave, only to become significant again in the ensuing wave. Based on these uneven findings, we concluded that our measures of impairment were not valid and were giving us little more than random results.

In search of answers, we returned to the original survey responses on illnesses and surgery since the last survey wave. By comparing actual survey responses we confirmed our worst fears about the data—the impairment codes, though based on high rater agreement, were not indicating true patterns of impairment. For example, when we compared the original survey responses of two men with so-called muscular-skeletal problems, we found very different health conditions. One reported a "sprained hand," the other "paralysis." In another pair of cases, a man reported mild ulcer symptoms that led him to restrict his diet; the other case required ulcer surgery. Both were coded "ulcer" despite the wide variation in disease severity. Such examples made it clear that we were working with inadequate indicators of impairment, and no manipulation of the existing codes would correct the basic problem.

STEP 2: THE DECISION TO RECODE

In the next step, we reevaluated the materials, including the original survey responses, to determine whether or not creating new health codes would be fruitful. Our final decision to recast the health data involved three major questions:

1. Did the original survey responses contain enough information for us to create better health codes than already existed, and did we have adequate access to these data?
2. Did the health data have limitations that could not be overcome?
3. What were the strengths of this archive in terms of understanding health, and were there ways to maximize the data's potential?

Based on earlier observation, we knew that the original survey responses offered major advantages over the existing health codes. The questions on illness/surgery were open-ended and included additional space for the respondent to elaborate. Similarly, the question about tendencies toward emotional problems provided several lines for respondents to add details. The emotional health question asked specifically for the date and nature of these problems, how they were handled, and the respondent's present condition. Our examination of case files told us that respondents were knowledgeable and candid about their health, often providing extensive details about important health problems. The qualitative materials contained detailed and often vivid physical and emotional histories that existing codes failed to capture, as well as substantial diversity in men's illness experiences.

Permission had generously been granted by the Terman Study director for access to the original files at Stanford. However, a major recoding effort would be labor- and time-intensive and the substantial distance between North Carolina and California presented a significant problem. Fortunately, staff members from the University of North Carolina at Chapel Hill had gone to Stanford to obtain copies of case materials for work and military histories. Thus we had on hand original information for each respondent, including partial surveys, letters to and from respondents, reports, newspapers, and transcribed interviews. This subset of materials included original responses to health questions for 1945, 1960, 1972, 1977, and 1986. When we combined this information with the secondary data on computer tape (e.g., date of death, general physical health), we concluded that it was sufficient to develop extensive health codes without returning to Stanford.

A second set of issues concerned limitations of the health data. Were there problems with the original data that could not be overcome, even with the careful development of new codes? For example, self-reports constituted our primary source of health information, thereby forcing heavy reliance on the respondents' ability and desire to explicate the often personal details of their physical and emotional functioning. Previous research in this area suggests that self-reports of general health condition are reliable predictors of physical health and mortality, particularly if comparisons are made between people of the same sex and cultural background (Idler & Kasl, 1991; Maddox & Douglass, 1973). The homogeneous nature of the Terman sample, including high levels of education, made us more confident about the reliability of combining self-reports and more specific health questions. We soon learned that the majority of Terman men were well informed about their health problems and often provided in great detail the symptomatology, clinical diagnosis, and medical management of conditions such as cancer or heart disease.

In addition to our concern about relying primarily on self-reports, we were aware that the wording of questions varied slightly across survey waves, and that there were several long periods between survey waves. The seriousness of these problems could be evaluated only when weighed against the strengths of the archive. Did the strengths outweigh these limitations, or would another data source better meet our needs?

The Terman archive provides more than 60 years of longitudinal data, allowing the researcher to look at antecedents and long-term consequences of health problems, including measures of military experiences in World War II. Richly detailed case histories include extensive information on factors that potentially affect health outcomes, including personal background, marriage and family life, work life and job satisfaction, avocational and volunteer activities, and life satisfaction. Furthermore, these case histories are combined with an adequate sample size to allow quantitative as well as qualitative analyses. Finally, while the wording of some survey questions changes over time, most of the health measures and other indicators are comparable from one survey wave to the next.

These strengths offered an unparalleled opportunity to examine the complex interactions between physical and emotional health and other factors in the lives of these men as they unfolded over a four-decade period. We concluded, therefore, that the assets of the archive far outweighed the limitations for examining patterns of health over time.

STEP 3: REFINING THE RESEARCH QUESTIONS

Our decision to recast the health data opened new potential for research ideas, returning us to the stage of conceptualizing our research questions. We felt strongly that the reformulated questions and new codes should be designed to build on the strengths of the archive rather than to disarm the weaknesses. Another major asset of the Terman archive, in addition to health and military data, is its detailed information on work and family lives throughout the adult years. Our new research questions could include these dimensions through exploration of relationships among health, work, and family over several decades. Because we had decided to recast the health data, we were in a position to formulate new questions that would allow us to examine health in ways unavailable from other types of survey data.

Strategies for analyzing changes in health over time and across individuals include panel, event history, and pooled time-series designs. However, our reading of the Terman case histories identified physical and emotional health *trajectories* over the course of life that were not captured by a simple look at change in health from one cross section to another. Though scientific knowledge about health trajectories is virtually nonexistent beyond the realm of clinical case studies, certain patterns in the Terman data were easily identified. For example, a large number of the men had relatively stable health histories. Of this group, some were endowed with superb physical or mental constitution and consequently manifested good or excellent health for most of their lives. By contrast, a smaller group appeared inherently frail, falling victim to illness or injury frequently. Other lives were characterized by changes in health status, subtle or pronounced.

Direction and slope of health changes seemed to correspond to illness severity, extent of recovery, and nature of deficits. For some, health declines were rare but did occur, as for a healthy individual who experienced a major heart attack with recovery in mid-life. In other instances, more frequent or sporadic declines corresponded to acute illness episodes (e.g., pneumonia, auto accident) or chronic problems (e.g., diabetes, arthritis).

Perhaps the most relevant introduction to the concept of health trajectory comes from the words of the participants in the Terman sample. The following excerpts were unsolicited, offered by participants at various points in adulthood and old age. "I've been blessed with good health all my life." "My health was great until the heart attack in 1962 . . . but I fully recovered." "My health has never been what you'd call good, even as a child." "I've always been a nervous type, a worrier." "After my illness [cancer] I had to retire . . . now I have to limit myself." "I've suffered from depressions off and on for years." These statements reflect ongoing physical and emotional processes. Each captures movement across time and health states. Each sketches out a trajectory (Figure 3.2).

Based on these observations, we developed new questions on the dynamics of health across adulthood and later life. What are the major trajectories of physical and emotional health most individuals follow over time? What are the background factors and medical conditions associated with various trajectories? To what extent do the trajectories of physical and emotional health correspond to each other, and under what conditions do they differ? Finally, how do people with different trajectories (e.g., men who experience a decline and recovery versus those in constant good health) differ from one another, and what factors are most closely associated with those differences?

A second set of research questions builds on the richness of the archive to model the complex interactions between health and other aspects of men's lives. We were particularly interested in how aspects of work and family life affect health. Can we identify links between family and/or work events, such as job promotions or marital status changes, and physical and emotional health? Do health effects of these events vary by life stage? How does career and family success influence long-term health and mortality? Exploration of these questions makes full use of the detailed histories of health, family, and career available in the Terman archive.

A final set of research questions relates to our initial interest in military service and health, but also builds on the greater flexibility promised by new health codes. In addition to a capacity to assess

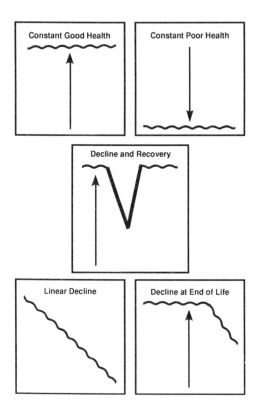

Figure 3.2. Physical Health Trajectories

general health effects of military service, we are now in a position to examine emotional or behavioral problems more specifically, as in the case of anxiety, depression, ulcers, and alcoholism. Did military service or combat duty increase the likelihood that men would experience these symptoms? If so, did they experience them immediately after the war or several years later?

These three broad areas of health research (individual trajectories, health and career/family, health and military service) demonstrate the full value of our decision to recast the health data. The new data potentially seem to offer more reliable health measures, and in doing so significantly increase our ability to answer new and exciting questions about health processes.

In the next section we describe the necessary steps we followed in translating the concepts into reliable measures. Continuing with the health example, we present a method to organize the data within a particular domain and then offer guidelines for creating a codebook and coding form. We conclude with a discussion of interrater reliability and its assessment.

Creating New Codes

STEP 4: EVALUATING AVAILABLE CODING SCHEMES

A unique aspect of recasting an archive is that new concepts are defined and operationalized long after data have been collected. This may mean that standard measures drawn from relevant literatures must be adapted to correspond to available information, or perhaps that new measures have to be derived. Although this issue was briefly addressed in the discussion of evaluating the strengths and limitations of the data, it is at this stage of the project when researchers must decide whether to adapt a standardized coding scheme to their needs or to develop entirely new codes.

In making this decision, several questions must be addressed. First, is there an existing coding scheme that would allow the research questions to be answered? In our health project, measures of physical and emotional health as well as the more specific emotional/behavioral condition (anxiety, depression, ulcers, alcoholism) could be partially based on standardized measures, but the concept of health trajectory was completely new and had to be based entirely on the data at hand. Second, do preexisting codes fit the available data? Survey questions developed years ago are not likely to be the same as those developed for contemporary studies, and even concepts that fit the data fairly well may have to be adapted to take account of questionnaire differences. In either case, when working with an archive, one should expect to move back and forth many times among the concepts, measures, and data.

In our health example, we encountered a major barrier to using standardized measures as more than a basic guideline. Many measures of health in the literature are based on recent data collections designed to extract very specific information, including long checklists that prompt respondents to address a wide range of potential health problems. By contrast, questions in the Terman archive were designed to gather general health information and relied heavily on open-ended queries, leading to much greater variation in the types of responses given. As a result, we would need to design relatively general measures of physical and mental impairment that could make full use of all types of information—general and specific—respondents provided.

Having decided to design new codes, the researcher's next step is to inventory the data thoroughly. A summary sheet for each respondent provides a standardized framework for reviewing each case, extracting all information relevant to a domain of interest (e.g., health), and organizing this information in one place. Although time-consuming, completing the summary sheet familiarizes the researcher with the data and serves as a valuable resource in future research. In fact, we have found summary sheets to be so valuable that we complete them as part of the coding operation even when relying on a standardized scheme.

In our health example, we initially thought we could rely on standardized codes, and thus filled in a summary sheet as we coded each case. However, the process of completing the summary sheets helped us develop and refine our concepts of health so substantially that we needed to define new concepts and code each case a second time. For example, we encountered unanticipated symptom patterns related to depression, anxiety, and alcohol consumption. Only after a full inventory of all case files did we have a true sense of the range of health information and illness patterns that men reported. Thus our second coding supplemented the first set of codes and increased the precision with which we defined health states and captured health dynamics. Other coding operations may be able to rely more successfully on preexisting codes (see the later work-life example in Chapter 4) and thus the researcher can combine the two steps of completing the summary sheet and doing the actual coding.

The design of the summary sheet depends on what information is to be extracted from the case files. Regardless of substantive area (e.g., health, creativity, fertility, work), the investigator needs to record and organize all information relevant to that domain. Because of our theoretical interest in temporal processes and the life course, we used survey year and the three repeated measures of self-reported health to organize each individual's health history. Figure 3.3 is an example of a completed summary sheet. Note how these key pieces of information quickly summarize health at one point as well as temporal patterns of health. Each row of the summary sheet records the multiple indicators of health included at a survey wave, while each column records any one indicator over the four decades.

ID NUMBER <u>0515</u>

HEALTH SUMMARY SHEET

YEAR	General Physical Condition	Emotional Disturbances	Illnesses & Operations
1945	*very good*	*none*	*colds* *1950-high blood pressure-no tx*
1960	*good* *moderate drinker*	*none*	*1955-tx for high blood pressure* *1957-stroke*
1972	*good* *adequate energy*	*none*	*none*
1977	*good* *adequate energy*	*none* *very happy*	*high blood pressure, tx*
1982	*missing*		
1986	Decline in: hearing ____ vision ____ health ____ musc. strength & control ____	*missing*	

1953 divorced .
1957 forced retirement due to serious illness
1962 re entered practice
Also says "Ages 54-58 recuperating from massive
stroke in 1957, 10 days in coma and completely
paralyzed"

Figure 3.3. Example of Health Summary Sheet

The case we present (Figure 3.3) illustrates the importance of the additional information gained by recasting. If we rely only on this man's evaluation of his general physical condition, he appears to have had constant good health from 1945 to 1977. But his reports of illnesses and surgery tell a more complete story. We learn that he was treated for high blood pressure and stroke in 1957, but seems to have recovered fully by 1960. Only through his work history do we realize the severity of his stroke. Asked about work in the 1977 survey, the respondent indicated that he had to retire temporarily for four years. Asked about life turning points in the same survey, he replied that he was in a coma for 10 days. We gain insight into not only the severity of this man's illness, but also his ability to recover, since he was finally able to return to work and remained in good health through 1977. Instead of "constant good health," as indicated by his self-reports, this man clearly had one episode of severe impairment followed by recovery. Information on date or cause of death would be recorded in the appropriate time slot.

STEP 5: WRITING THE CODEBOOK

After summary sheets have been completed and concepts have been clearly defined from them, the next step is to document each code in the codebook. As with previous steps, writing the codebook involves a long process of moving back and forth among research question, measures, and data to refine the definition of each code. The completed codebook should include the following:

1. a full description of the archive and its contents, including background information on research goals behind the recoding effort;
2. concept definitions and substantive examples of each code; and
3. decision rules for coding each variable.

We found clear documentation of the data in the health-coding project especially important because decisions were based on a subset of the full case file, which future data users would need to take into account.

The core of the codebook consists of variable definitions, corresponding codes, and examples for each code. Our measure of physical health for each survey year appears in Table 3.3. At the top of the page we list the variable name and concept definition. This measure is based primarily on the self-reports of general physical condition and any mentions of illness, accidents, and surgery. Additional information relating to physical health (e.g., alcoholism) is included in our evaluation. The new physical health code has the same four-point scale as the existing self-rating, but adds more specific information on illness from respondents' reports. For example, we code someone in "good" physical health if the report specifies acute resolvable conditions (a fractured wrist) or mild chronic conditions (asthma).

Even the most straightforward and clearly defined measures will not fit each case perfectly. Consequently, a final and crucial part of the codebook involves the development of decision rules that deal with ambiguous cases systematically. Case 515 (Figure 3.3) provides a good example of the need for decision rules. This report of general physical

39

TABLE 3.3
Defining the Codes: Example Page From Health Codebook

PHLT45S2-PHLT82S2 = self-reported physical health in survey year
(based on all health information)
Variable Name   *Codes/Examples*

Variable Name	Codes/Examples
PHLT45S2 PHLT60S2 PHLT72S2 PHLT77S2 PHLT82S2	2 = *Excellent*: no reported problems, no evidence of problems except extremely minor mentions of colds, mild allergies, etc., that all persons usually experience. 3 = *Good*: acute resolvable conditions or mild chronic conditions, but not physical health impairments. Examples: broken arm, hemorrhoidectomy, other isolated injuries; pneumonia, chronic bronchitis, asthma, hernia repair, high blood pressure possibly requiring medication but with no other complications, prostate operation with no complications, "stomach trouble" or ulcer requiring no treatment, benign tumor removal, minor skin cancer treatment, minor headaches, arthritis, minor sensory deficits. 4 = *Fair*: definite physical health impairment present, chronic conditions or significant acute episodes. Examples: minor heart attack, moderate accident or injury, diabetes, ulcer surgery, isolated cancer surgery (e.g., polyps), gall bladder surgery, minor stroke, alcoholism, lupus, severe high blood pressure causing limitations, nonobstructive emphysema, severe arthritis with evidence of limitations, herpes zoster with impairment, severe headaches, significant sensory deficits with obvious uncorrectable impairments (e.g., can't drive, blindness). 5 = *Poor*: physical health severely impaired, prognosis may be grave. Examples: lung cancer, leukemia, massive stroke or heart attack, metastatic cancer, cirrhosis of the liver, Alzheimer's disease, gastrointestinal bleeding, emphysema, or knowledge of an illness resulting in death in that year or soon after. 9 = *Missing survey* (including dead).

Rules:

If report of general physical condition does not correspond to illnesses or to emotional disturbances, code as lowest level of health reported. Examples: R reports "fair" general condition, with no illnesses or emotional problems, code physical health as "fair"; R reports "very good" general condition, but reports that he has high blood pressure and is on medication, code physical health as "good."

If R dies in survey year, judge degree of morbidity in that year, not mortality. Thus, if death is from a sudden event such as an accident, heart attack, or stroke without any evidence of a prolonged illness, do not include the event in your assessment of morbidity.

condition does not correspond with that for illnesses and surgery; in 1960, the respondent claimed he was in good physical health, even though he was still not working because of his stroke. The decision rule for coding such discrepancies is listed at the bottom of Table 3.3—we are to code the lowest level of health reported. In this case, the lowest level of health is indicated by the respondent's inability to work in 1960 because of a stroke suffered in 1957. In 1960, he had recovered somewhat from his stroke, but was still physically impaired in terms of role function, so, based on our new coding scheme, we code him in fair health in 1960.

STEP 6: CODING THE CASE

Once the data on a specific domain have been transferred from case files to summary sheets and the codes and decision rules have been defined, coding can begin. The process entails a precoding or test period followed by the actual coding. The precoding phase identifies further problems with variable definitions and decision rules and provides an opportunity for the investigator to view codes in their final form. For example, not until we precoded the health variables and reviewed the summary sheets did we incorporate the kinds of conditions frequently mentioned by respondents as examples in our codebook. We have found that as many as 10-20% of the cases may need to be precoded prior to the actual coding phase.

As each case is coded, values are recorded on a form listing each variable name followed by space for the proper code. This form should be customized to project needs and should also be easy to fill out and read, because accuracy of the final data largely depends on the clarity of the coding form. The code form is also an important final checkpoint for evaluating the new coding scheme, since it shows how data will look when entered into the computer. Do the codes, as they appear on this form, adequately capture the richness of the summary sheet? Are they in the correct form for desired data analyses *and* are they flexible enough for other types of analysis? If not, the coding scheme needs to be reevaluated and perhaps redesigned to meet the goals of the research.

Figure 3.4 is an example of the coding form for the health project, with title and case identification number at the top of the page. Each variable is listed with an adequate number of blanks to accommodate the appropriate codes. Variables are organized into sets that correspond to topical areas. Spacing the variable sets increases the ease of transferring the codes to the code sheet. In the health example, the top of the page includes all general physical and emotional health variables for

```
                                    ID#  __ __ __ __
            HEALTH CODES, TERMAN MEN 1945-1986

              PHLT45S2 ____         EHLT45S2 ____
 (1940-52)    PHLT45I2 ____         EHLT45I2 ____
              PHLT60S2 ____         EHLT60S2 ____
 (1953-66)    PHLT60I2 ____         EHLT60I2 ____
              PHLT72S2 ____         EHLT72S2 ____
 (1967-74)    PHLT72I2 ____         EHLT72I2 ____
              PHLT77S2 ____         EHLT77S2 ____
 (1975-77)    PHLT77I2 ____         EHLT77I2 ____
              PHLT82S2 ____         EHLT82S2 ____
 (1978-82)    PHLT82I2 ____         EHLT82I2 ____
```

ANX402 ____	DEP402 ____	ULCER402 ____
ANX532 ____	DEP532 ____	ULCER532 ____
ANX672 ____	DEP672 ____	ULCER672 ____
ANX752 ____	DEP752 ____	ULCER752 ____
ANX782 ____	DEP782 ____	ULCER782 ____
ALCSEV2 ____	WARPHYS2 ____	ERESPR2 ____
ALCAGE2 ____	WAREMOT2 ____	ERESGD2 ____
PHLTHIS2 ____	EHLTHIS2 ____	
PTX2 __ __	PTX2 __ __	

Figure 3.4. Health Project Coding Form

each time period, while the bottom half of the page includes codes for more specific variables, including anxiety, depression, ulcers, alcohol use, wartime experience, emotional resiliency, physical and emotional health trajectories, and the number of professional consultations for physical and emotional problems. The format should correspond to the order of variables in the codebook.

A final stage in coding the case is that of transferring the codes from the coding form to a computer file. The primary objectives in data entry are accuracy and efficiency, and all data should be entered twice to check for accurate entry. At the time of coding, we found SPSS/PC DE to be the most flexible program; it includes a wide range of features, such as verification of values entered, ability to set up the screen easily to match the coding form, and options for defining "skip and fill" rules to increase efficiency when the data include skip patterns.

STEP 7: ASSESSING RELIABILITY AND VALIDITY

Interrater reliability. The quality of new data depends on how reliably the codes were assigned, and it can be evaluated by comparing the degree of agreement between two or more coders. One rule of thumb is to calculate agreement between coders on a randomly selected 10% sample of all the cases. The choice among several available statistics for calculating agreement depends primarily on the metric of the variables being coded.

When the recoded variables are categorical (two or more categories), an appropriate statistic is kappa (Cohen, 1968; Fleiss, 1973). Kappa is preferable to chi-square and percentage agreement because it strictly measures agreement, whereas the other statistics include all types of association. Kappa is also preferable because it corrects for chance agreement, especially important when the marginal distributions in a table are highly skewed. The formula for kappa with two coders is as follows:

$$\kappa = \frac{(\text{overall agreement} - \text{chance agreement})}{(1 - \text{chance agreement})}.$$

Based on part A of Table 3.4,

$$\text{overall agreement} = \frac{(a + f + k + p)}{T}$$

and

$$\text{chance agreement} =$$

$$\frac{\dfrac{(\text{row 1})(\text{col 1})}{T} + \dfrac{(\text{row 2})(\text{col 2})}{T} + \dfrac{(\text{row 3})(\text{col 3})}{T} + \dfrac{(\text{row 4})(\text{col 4})}{T}}{T}$$

Kappa ranges from -1 to $+1$. If $\kappa = 0$, agreement between the coders is not better than chance. If $\kappa < 0$, agreement is less than chance. If $\kappa > 0$, agreement is better than chance. The precise statistical significance of κ can be determined by calculating its standard error and determining a z score (see Fleiss, 1973), although a general rule of thumb is that a

TABLE 3.4
Calculating the Kappa Statistic

A. Basic Kappa Table for a Four-Category Variable, Two Coders

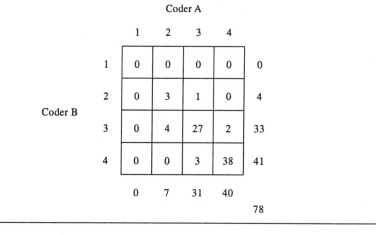

Coder A

		1	2	3	4	
	1	a	b	c	d	row 1
	2	e	f	g	h	row 2
Coder B	3	i	j	k	l	row 3
	4	m	n	o	p	row 4
		col 1	col 2	col 3	col 4	
						T

B. Kappa table for physical health in 1945, two coders

Coder A

		1	2	3	4	
	1	0	0	0	0	0
	2	0	3	1	0	4
Coder B	3	0	4	27	2	33
	4	0	0	3	38	41
		0	7	31	40	
						78

range of .2 to .4 indicates fair agreement, .4 to .6 moderate agreement, .6 to .8 substantial agreement, and .8 to 1.0 almost perfect agreement (Landis & Koch, 1977).

In the health example, we conducted nine reliability checks at equal intervals throughout the coding operation, totaling more than 10% of the 856 cases. Our two coders coded each case independently at each reliability check. The codes for each variable were cross-tabulated. As an example, part B of Table 3.4 demonstrates the final tabulation for physical health in 1945. Twelve cases had missing data, reducing the total (T) from 90 to 78. Missing cases were excluded for this variable because the determination of missing data was straightforward. For other variables, the decision to declare data "missing" required coder judgment, and in these cases, missing data (in this case a code of 9) are included in the final tabulation.

Using the formula above,

$$\text{overall agreement} = \frac{(0 + 3 + 27 + 38)}{78} = .87$$

$$\text{chance agreement} = \frac{\dfrac{0 \times 0}{78} + \dfrac{4 \times 7}{78} + \dfrac{33 \times 31}{78} + \dfrac{41 \times 40}{78}}{78} = .44$$

making

$$\kappa = \frac{.87 - .44}{1 - .44} = .77$$

According to Landis and Koch's (1977) standards, our level of agreement is "substantial," a conclusion confirmed by calculation of the standard error and z value (Fleiss, 1973). Overall, kappas for the health measures ranged from 1.0 to .69, with an average of .87.

Kappa can be generalized to other research designs. Reliability checks for ordinal variables can be computed using weighted kappa if certain pairs of ratings show substantial disagreement (some disagreements are clearly worse than others) (Cohen, 1968; Spitzer, Cohen, Fleiss, & Endicott, 1967). Weighted kappa requires assigning weights to each cell, which are then incorporated into the basic kappa formula. One of the limitations of using weighted kappa is that there are no preset standards for determining the weights. In fact, weighted kappa would be appropriate for the physical health variable presented above, but without theoretical rationale for assigning weights, the additional complications of weighting the categories outweighed any potential gain. Kappa can also be generalized to designs with more than two raters (Fleiss, 1971; Light, 1971).

When the variable being coded is continuous, it is more important that small differences in opinion between coders be considered less severe than large differences. For this reason, the intraclass correlation coefficient (ICC) is more appropriate than kappa for intercoder reliability assessment of continuous variables (Fleiss, 1973; Robinson, 1957). In its most basic form, the ICC is derived from a one-way analysis of variance design. It is preferable to the Pearson correlation because the ICC assesses only pure agreement, whereas the Pearson correlation coefficient depicts any form of linear relationship between coders (Robinson, 1957).

To compute the ICC, one first computes a one-way analysis of variance model with k raters on a sample of n persons (for greater detail, see Bartko, 1966; Burdock, Fleiss, & Hardesty, 1963). The resulting ANOVA table summarizes the variance components into mean squares between groups (in this case, coders) and mean squares error. The estimate of the ICC can then be calculated as follows:

$$ICC = \frac{(MS_{between} - MS_{error})}{[MS_{between} + (k-1)MS_{error}]}$$

The test of significance of the ICC is computed using the F statistic

$$F = \frac{MS_{between}}{MS_{error}},$$

with $n - 1$ and $n(k - 1)$ degrees of freedom (Bartko, 1966).

In Table 3.5, we illustrate how the ICC is calculated based on examples from Ebel (1951) and Bartko (1966). In this example there are two raters and four subjects. The second part of the table displays the standard analysis of variance, and from this we calculate

$$ICC = \frac{(4.167 - 3.250)}{[4.167 + (1)3.250]} = 0.1236.$$

Based on the formula above, $F = 1.28$, so the ICC, and thus interrater agreement, is nonsignificant at the .05 level. If the ICC were high, it would indicate very little residual variation that might affect coding decisions (Burdock et al., 1963).

This basic formula for the ICC assesses the overall reliability of the instrument, but assumes that the coders are fixed and there is no

TABLE 3.5
Analysis of Interrater Agreement With the Intraclass
Correlation Coefficient

A. Data of Interrater Agreement With Four Subjects and Two Coders

Subjects	Coders 1	2	Σ
1	3	3	6
2	1	5	6
3	5	6	11
4	4	7	11
E	13	21	34

B. Analysis of Variance

Source	df	SS	MS	F
Between	3	12.5	4.167	1.28
Error	4	13.0	3.250	
Total	7	25.5		

Source: Data and example from Bartko (1966), Ebel (1951).

interaction between them and cases (Burdock et al., 1963). Further information on variation between coders or coder-by-case interactions can be attained by modifying the analysis of variance design and making appropriate adjustments to the ICC formula (Bartko, 1966; Burdock et al., 1963).

Criterion and construct validity. The final step of coding involves checking the validity of the new codes. We began by determining the criterion validity—the degree of association between new measures and other more established indicators of the concept (Bailey, 1978). In the health example, we compared physical health trajectories with other indicators of physical health, such as primary illness that affected the respondent's life, and energy and vitality in the later years. Our primary interest in making these comparisons is to determine whether the health information is consistent across different measures, even though each measure captures a different aspect of health.

Each of the five trajectories (Figure 3.2) represents health in terms of a unique combination of illness versus wellness and stability versus change. "Constant good" and "constant poor" health are relatively stable patterns. In our study, constant good health was the most common profile, with 36%

of the men falling into this category. By contrast, only 3% of the men remained in poor physical health throughout their adult lives. Among men who experienced significant health changes, most were either healthy throughout their adult lives and then declined shortly before death (25%) or experienced one or more declines and recoveries (22%). Among the change patterns, linear decline represents the most prolonged episode of poor health, and only 14% of the men fall into this category.

Each health trajectory may be related to the absence or presence of a variety of physical health problems; some are more suggestive of certain illnesses than others. For example, men with heart disease are more likely to decline and recover or steadily decline, while men with cancer may be less likely to recover and so decline quickly at the end of their lives.

In part A of Figure 3.5, we confirm our expectations that many health trajectories are highly associated with disease categories. Among men whose primary health problem is heart disease, 31% recovered after the initial problem, 26% slowly declined without recovery, and 23% declined more rapidly at the end of life. By contrast, only 15% of men with cancer recovered, while 69% declined at the end of life. Men with a chronic disease such as diabetes most likely either experienced a slow, linear decline (35%) or decline and improvement (28%).

Measures of energy and vitality in the later years provide a different kind of health comparison. Chronic diseases are captured in the illness category measure. By contrast, measures of energy and vitality reveal an aspect of well-being captured at only one point in the life course. We expect some patterns, such as constant good health, constant poor health, or linear decline to be clearly associated with energy level. Patterns of decline and recovery and decline at the end of life, however, are likely to have less clear associations because declines may or may not correspond to the life stage when energy is being measured.

In part B of Figure 3.5, we find that energy and vitality are highly associated with some of the health trajectories, particularly those that represent the more stable health patterns. Men who stayed in constant good health throughout their lives were most likely also to report having vigorous or adequate energy, while only 1% of those in constant poor health reported adequate energy. At the other end of the scale, 31% of men who reported limited energy fit into the linear decline pattern, with another 9% in constant poor health. Energy and vitality are poorly associated with decline at the end of life, with men in this pattern equally likely to report having limited or vigorous energy. We suspect that the association depends highly on whether the decline occurred

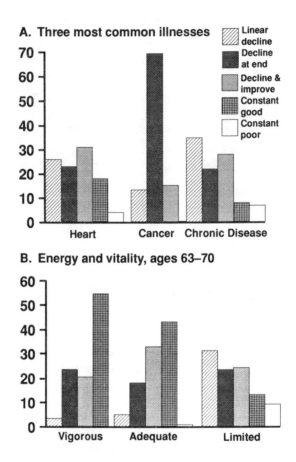

Figure 3.5. Physical Health Trajectories by Illness and Health States
NOTE: Missing categories for cancer and vigorous = 0.

between ages 63 and 70 or later in life. Men who had experienced decline and improvement were most likely to report inadequate energy, suggesting that while they had recovered, their health setbacks had taken a toll on their energy levels.

Overall, these comparisons make much intuitive sense. They suggest that health trajectories are valid measures that provide a unique view of health, consistent with other health measures. Further analyses of relationships between health trajectories and other variables, such as education and marital history, provide additional evidence of construct validity. Men with advanced degrees were more likely to be in constant good health, while those with only high school educations were more likely to have had linear health decline or to be in constant poor health. Similarly, men with intact marriages throughout most of their lives tended to be in constant good health, while those in constant poor health tended to remain single. The causal mechanisms between these variables still need to be explored, but the strong associations are consistent with well-established relationships between health and social factors, thus confirming the internal validity of our newly created measures.

Summary

We have detailed the ordered phases in the process of recasting an archive. Figure 3.1 best describes the decision process, showing phases of recasting common to all secondary data analysis and specific to archival data. The step-by-step recasting process is illustrated through the creation of new health codes for men in the Terman sample. We next illustrate how the process applies to other domains in the Terman archive—work patterns in later life and wartime experience.

4. FROM RETIREMENT TO LATE-LIFE CAREERS

With each recoding effort the researcher is faced with slightly different issues requiring changes in the recoding process. Our recoding of men's work in later life closely paralleled the health project, but differed because we could build on preexisting codes for industry and occupation. In this chapter, we illustrate how the recoding process outlined in Chapter 3 can be applied to a project guided by a different set of conceptual issues and built on standardized codes.

First Approach

STEP 1: EVALUATION OF EXISTING MATERIALS

Our initial interest in work in later life was guided by two questions about the long-term effects of World War II on work lives. Did time out of the labor force for military service directly delay retirement while

50

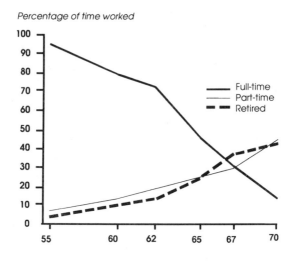

Figure 4.1. Percentage of Men Working Full-Time, Part-Time, and Retired in 1977, by Age

men made up the years of work missed? Were there any long-term, indirect effects of military service on earnings or career success that altered the timing of men's retirement?

Before these questions could be answered, fundamental changes in the occupation codes were necessary. As with other data in the Terman archive, occupation had been coded separately with each survey, resulting in a series of cross-sectional codes. An additional problem was that the coding scheme had changed over the years, making individual work-life histories and long-term comparisons of occupation impossible to attain. An earlier project had used 1980 census occupation codes to create yearly work records from first job to 1960, but this effort needed to be extended to include occupations after 1960.

Occupational histories of the Terman men presented an even greater problem as we began to think about issues of retirement. Many men did not retire by leaving the work force at a point in time, or if they did retire, they often continued working for pay in some capacity long after their official "retirement." Figure 4.1 illustrates this complexity. As expected, at age 55, most men worked full-time, but with each year the percentage working full-time dropped steadily. Most surprising is that, for all ages, the percentage of men working part-time nearly parallels the percentage who are fully retired. Thus, in this sample, part-time work was as much a reality for many men as was full retirement.

Considerations of part-time work raised further questions about work patterns in later life. What were these men doing? Were they retiring from one job and then working part-time elsewhere, or did their part-time work represent a process of slowly phasing out work before retirement? Did part-time work represent a major portion of their time, and how long did they tend to work in such a capacity? The overall percentages in Figure 4.1 cannot answer these questions; we need to look at individual work histories to gain some understanding of how men worked and retired in their later years. The Terman archive offers a unique opportunity to do this, since it contains work histories over entire adult lives.

Our initial reading of the case files offered a stark contrast to conventional notions that later-life work is a relatively stable process and that the major transition is retirement, a single exit from the labor force. Men in our sample tended to have varied work changes after age 50—some were between closely related jobs, while others were moves to vastly different occupations. Reductions and increases in time worked were quite common. For some, these changes were associated with "retirement" from one job, but often they were not. Overall, there was great variety in what men did in later life.

The graphs in Figure 4.2 display some of this variability. Graph A shows the stereotypical pattern of work and retirement for a man who worked for a large insurance company most of his adult life. At age 50, he is promoted to group manager of the firm, works full-time until age 62, then retires fully. Two patterns of part-time work after retirement appear in graphs B and C. In graph B, an engineer works full-time until he retires at age 56. He continues working part-time as a consultant for the same company, slowly reducing his time over a 10-year period, so that he does not exit the labor force until age 66. Graph C shows a man who works full-time at the Social Security Administration until age 59. Immediately after retirement, he is a substitute teacher for 2 years, putting in just over half-time. At age 61 he becomes a paint salesman. In the first year, he works 1 or 2 days a week, dropping to less than a day a week in the second year. At 64, he stops working for pay.

The work histories in graphs D-F complicate the issue of retirement even further, given that in each case it is questionable whether retirement can be characterized as a single transition. Graph D depicts a lawyer who leaves a general-practice firm for self-employment at age 55. He does not indicate that this change is a retirement or list any

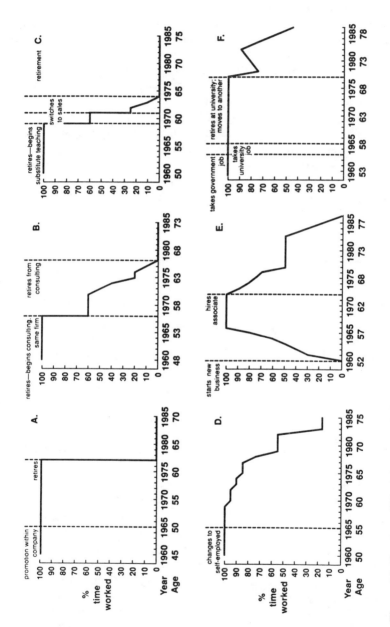

Figure 4.2. Patterns of Work in Later Life

52

pension information to indicate "retiring" from the firm. He works full-time until age 59, then gradually reduces his work time. At 75, he still practices law about six hours a week.

The work pattern of a self-employed businessman appears in graph E. Having launched a successful business, this man sells it and retires before age 50. In 1960 he opens a contracting and retailing firm, slowly increasing his work effort until he returns to full-time work at 57. At 64, he hires an associate and begins slowly to reduce his work time, but does not stop entirely until after age 75. Graph F shows the work life of a university professor who is heavily involved in international consulting. After two major transitions in his late 50s, he maintains his primary affiliation with a major university until "retirement" at age 70. He continues in much the same capacity, however, moving to another university and continuing international work throughout his 70s. At age 79 this professor is still working close to half-time.

These patterns of later-life work raise a number of conceptual and methodological questions about retirement. First, given the extent of part-time work in this sample, how should we define and measure retirement? Is retirement a job transition, a reduction in time worked, or defined by some other criterion, such as receipt of a pension? Probably any single definition will apply to some work patterns more than others. For example, defining retirement as a job transition does not apply well to those who slowly reduce their time worked in the same job. However, relying on time worked as an indicator, such as defining people as "retired" once they drop below half-time, does not acknowledge the major work transitions where one "retires" from one job but moves directly into another. Thus it may be that no single measure can fully capture the range of work-life experiences in the sample.

Beyond problems of definition and measurement, the apparent variation in the sample raises a more conceptual question. Analyses of "retirement" make an underlying assumption that a single event best characterizes later-life work. Thus the later years of work are assumed to be relatively stable and orderly, with the major change being an exit out of the labor force. Our reading of the case files suggests that these assumptions of stability apply only to a small subset of respondents. For many others, work in later life is a very dynamic process—a time of great change. These changes may involve exploring new kinds of work as well as reductions in time worked. To understand fully the factors that shape this process, we must address not only the transitions, but the overall context of the work history in which they are embedded.

STEP 2: THE DECISION TO RECODE

Having decided that we needed to focus more broadly on the entire pattern of work in later life, we took the next step, evaluating the data. A major concern was whether respondents were asked enough questions about their work in the later surveys to allow us to reconstruct job histories. We were pleased to find that in the 1972 and 1977 surveys, the men were explicitly asked to list their current occupations and nature of work and dates and nature of any job changes since the previous survey. In addition, several surveys included a time line for listing the percentage of time worked in every year since age 50. Many questions concerned information that overlapped with previous surveys, allowing for checks on the reliability of subjects' responses. This basic information was often supplemented with resumés, newspaper clippings, and even obituaries describing work histories. Thus even though the data had not been coded as work histories, there were enough data for us to reconstruct those histories for the men reliably.

As with any secondary data, there were also limitations that forced us to think carefully about the kinds of questions we would and would not be able to answer. One major concern was that in 1982 and 1986, the men were asked explicitly about the amounts of time worked, but not their occupations. Many were still working full- or part-time in 1982, and while many indicated the nature of their jobs, we could not assume that work information was complete in the later years. Another problem was that questions on important factors that might influence work decisions, such as pensions and mandatory retirement, were asked only in 1977. Thus, when analyzing job transitions after 1977, we could not account for the influence of these factors.

Despite these limitations, the archive still offered the potential for analysis of work histories from first job until later life for the men, letting us consider broad patterns of work and individual transitions. Rich data on military experience, health, education, and family would allow many comparisons among different facets of men's lives. However, we needed to refine our initial research questions on the long-term effects of the war on work and retirement substantially if we were to build on the vast strengths of the archive as well as to account for its weaknesses.

STEP 3: REFINING THE RESEARCH QUESTIONS

A major conceptual change brought about by our decision to recode was the change in emphasis from retirement to later-life careers. While many studies have examined aspects of gradual or partial retirement (e.g. Fillenbaum & Maddox, 1974; Fuchs, 1982; Gustman & Steinmeier, 1984; Honig & Hanoch, 1985; Myers, 1991), few have examined individual work-life patterns. Given this lack of information, our first research task centered on describing the trajectories and transitions these men followed as they entered their later years. What were the major patterns of work in our sample, and how were the men distributed among them? What percentage of men "retired" in a single transition? What percentage reduced their time slowly, and how many left and reentered the labor force? Finally, within each of these overall patterns, what did the individual transitions look like? How many transitions were there, and what percentage of men defined one or more of those transitions as a retirement?

After describing these patterns, we focused next on the task of determining which factors shape the direction of work lives. Occupation and self-employment clearly offer some people more flexibility than others, while income, pensions, and mandatory retirement policies provide opportunities or constraints for work in the later years. Beyond these, how do other factors—such as spouse's employment, health, and earlier work issues, such as military service—affect work lives? Our third task was to address the implications of the timing and shape of work trajectories for other patterns of aging. Does the pattern of work have any relationship to activity level, well-being, or longevity? These new research questions allow us to make full use of the strengths of the Terman archive, as they look at the relationships between work and other aspects of men's lives.

Creating New Codes

STEP 4: EVALUATING AVAILABLE CODING SCHEMES

In the health example (Chapter 3), we determined there was no existing coding scheme that would fit our data and meet our research needs. In coding late-life careers, several factors favored using U.S. Census Bureau occupation and industry codes as the basis for our new scheme. First, these codes were used for occupation prior to 1960, and changing to another scheme would require revising the earlier codes. Second, occupational information in the Terman archive consistently included questions about occupation and the nature of work, the essential information needed for census codes. Finally, detailed manuals on correct classification of occupation and industry are available from the Census Bureau. The decision to use a standardized coding scheme saved a vast amount of time, because we could avoid the step of making summary sheets, which requires reading and recording each case prior to the actual coding. Also, using a common coding scheme increases comparability with other studies.

Adapting a standard scheme to the demands of the research questions and the data requires several moves back and forth among the research questions, the coding scheme, and the data until the final scheme is complete. The first step is to establish specific recoding goals to ensure maximum fit between research questions and final codes. In recoding work in later life, a primary goal was to create new codes flexible enough to be adapted for future research projects. This meant thinking about all possible uses of the work-life data and attempting to create codes to meet these potential needs. Thus we decided to convert occupational data in each survey wave to 1980 census codes, even though our current research interests focused more on life-history data. In the long run, conversion of the cross-sectional data to census codes would continue our earlier efforts to apply a single, standardized occupational coding scheme to all occupational data in the archive. Once this was complete, users of the archive could easily compare occupations across survey waves, where previously they had to rely on different coding schemes over time.

To meet our more immediate research needs, we would also need to create codes for work transitions and trajectories. Beginning in 1960 (when the previous recoding effort stopped), we were interested in any change in employer, occupation, industry, or time worked as a transition. Within each transition, two components were of particular concern. First, we wanted to know about characteristics of the transition, such as when it occurred, if the respondent defined it as a retirement, and if it was directly related to a health change. Second, we needed relevant information on the new job (considering full retirement as a valid job state), including employer, industry, occupation, and time worked. This level of detail would allow us to analyze key transitions, such as those the subject defined as a retirement, or the whole pattern of transitions, possibly contrasting the total number of transitions or the range of occupations worked in the later years.

Because the overall trajectory of work held significant theoretical interest for us, we also wanted to develop some general measures that might not be easily obtained from the transition data. We were especially interested in the overall pattern of time worked, so that we could make broad comparisons among patterns such as a single retirement, slow reduction in time worked, and movement in and out of the labor force. Additional information about whether the respondent ever did consulting work, had a significant change in the type of work in his later years, or continued performing work-related tasks without pay after leaving the labor force could also be included here.

STEP 5: WRITING THE CODEBOOK

Having developed a general framework to meet our research interests, we initiated the iterative process of trying our preliminary codes on actual cases and revising the definitions and rules. If summary sheets are completed as a preliminary step, as with the health example, this process may be somewhat shortened because researchers become very familiar with the specific aspects of the data while completing the summary sheets. By contrast, when a preexisting scheme is used as a basis for new codes, this refinement process becomes a crucial step in achieving a good fit between concepts and data.

In our first attempt to check the preliminary codes, we randomly selected 20 cases. Any problems were fully documented, and after all cases had been coded, changes were made in the codebook. This initial process continued until 20-30 cases could be adequately coded with few or no problems. Next, we had three people unfamiliar with the project attempt to code a sample of cases. They were instructed to note any problems and ambiguities they encountered, and when completed, their responses were compared to assess the initial reliability of the codes. After further revisions were made, the actual coding could begin, although assessment and correction of any problems continued throughout the coding operation.

STEP 6: CODING THE CASE

One of the first steps in coding a case is to compile and organize all relevant data. If summary sheets have been made as a preliminary step, they can be used for this purpose. We did not complete summary sheets, but coders noted key work events and other relevant information while coding each case. These notations organize relevant information scattered throughout the file, document coding decisions, and serve as a useful reference for later use.

Figure 4.3 is an example of a completed coding form. The meaning of each code is defined in the codebook, but even without it, we can reconstruct the basic outline of this respondent's work history. The

ID NUMBER 0 0 6 8

CODED
ENTERED
VERIFIED
PROBLEM

Later Life Careers—Terman Men 1960-1986

Status/Death Date _living_
_b. 1910_

I. PRIMARY OCCUPATION: TIME POINTS

	EMP	IND	OCC	TIME	
1959	0 1	7 1 1	0 0 7	7	Comptroller, life insurance company
1972	0 1	7 1 1	0 1 9	7	V.P. & treasurer, same company
1977	0 8	7 1 2	2 5 4	3	Self-employed real estate broker 35% time

II. 1976 INCOME DATA

	EARNINC	SSINC	PENSINC	INVINC	JINVINC	OTHINC
1976	0 3 0 0	0 0 0 0	0 2 4 0	0 0 0 0	0 0 6 0	0 0 0 0

Figure 4.3. Example Coding Form for Late-Life Careers

III. TRANSITION IN PRIMARY OCCUPATION DURING AND AFTER 1959

		TRANSITION				NEW JOB			
	YEAR	AGE	RET	HEALTH	EMP	IND	OCC	TIME	
Trans #1	70	60	0	0	01	711	019	7	became V.P. same co.
Trans #2	72	62	1	0	08	710	255	7	self-emp. investments
Trans #3	72	62	0	0	08	712	254	5	" real estate broker 50% time
Trans #4	73	63	0	0	08	712	254	4	same - 40% time
Trans #5	75	65	0	0	08	712	254	3	" 35% time
Trans #6	84	74	0	0	08	712	254	1	" 15% time
Trans #7	—	—	—	—	—	—	—	—	
Trans #8	—	—	—	—	—	—	—	—	
Trans #9	—	—	—	—	—	—	—	—	
Trans #10	—	—	—	—	—	—	—	—	

CONFTRAN 2

IV. SUMMARY MEASURES

CONSULT	FCH	WORKTRAJ	CONT	ESTDATE	QUOTE	DIFFIC	CODER
1	1	1	1	1	0	2	5
		admin to sales					

Figure 4.3. Continued

59

coding scheme is divided into four sections. Occupation in each survey year and income data (available only for 1976) are listed on the first page. A quick glance indicates that this man, born in 1910, was still living in 1986. A comptroller for an insurance company in 1959, he had become vice president by 1972. By 1977, he was a self-employed real estate broker working just under two days a week.

The second page of the coding form includes codes for transitions, trajectories, and some checks on data quality. This man had six transitions between 1970 and 1984, including promotion to vice president of his company, retirement from that company, becoming a full-time investment broker, moving to part-time real estate work, then slowly reducing his work time so that at age 74 he worked less than a day a week. At the bottom of the transition section, a value of 2 for the variable CONFTRAN indicates that we are relatively certain this respondent had six transitions, plus or minus one.

The final section of the coding form includes several summary measures, including our measure for overall pattern of work time (WORKTRAJ). A code of 1 indicates that this man slowly reduced his work time. Other codes show that this man did some paid consulting before or after his retirement (CONSULT), that he had a functional change in occupation when he went from administration to sales (FCH), and that he continued some form of unpaid work after he began reducing his paid effort (CONT). Other codes provide further information on data quality, availability, and the coder for this case. As with the health example, a full-screen data-entry program was used so that the computer screen looked identical to the codeform, thus maximizing accuracy and efficiency.

STEP 7: ASSESSING RELIABILITY AND VALIDITY

Interrater reliability. After coding was complete, we could evaluate the reliability of the coding effort. Nine reliability checks had been conducted at even intervals throughout the coding scheme, totaling just over 10% of the sample. At each check, two coders independently assessed each case and their codes were then compared. At the end of the coding process, results from each reliability check were combined, and kappa statistics were calculated for each variable.

Results from the reliability estimates indicate a high level of interrater agreement. The mean kappa for the cross-sectional occupation, industry, and time measures was .84. Within this group, time worked in

1959 had a surprisingly low value of .35. Further examination of the data revealed that coder agreement on this variable was quite high (93%), but that because almost all men were working full-time in 1959, there was very little variation in the distribution, making chance agreement high also. In this case, instead of indicating unreliable codes, a low kappa reflects a highly skewed distribution.

Reliability estimates for income and event measures were just as promising, ranging from 1.0 to .72. Among the summary measures, whether a respondent had a functional change in occupation was the most difficult to code, and the kappa (.67) reflected this difficulty. Even this value was not alarmingly low, but, combined with the coders' concerns, it indicated our need to use the measure cautiously. Agreement was quite good for work-life trajectory (.79), consulting (.84), and continuity in paid to unpaid work (.81).

Validity. To check the validity of the new codes we compared overall patterns of work in later life with employment characteristics such as self-employment and occupation. Before turning to these comparisons, however, we first describe some basic aspects of work in later life that are newly accessible after our coding effort.

Overall, the Terman men averaged three transitions in employer, occupation, industry, or time worked between 1959 and 1986. By far, the largest percentage (28%) had one transition, but 8% had none and 22% had five or more. Narrowing our focus to transitions that respondents defined as retirements, we find that most men in our sample (62%) defined only one transition as a retirement, while 31% had no retirements and 7% retired two or more times.

Among those who did retire, we also find that many men continued working in some capacity after retirement. In our sample, 55% completely exited the labor force immediately after a self-defined retirement. Among the 45% who remained working, 25% continued working full-time, 14% continued working between half- and full-time, 29% worked between one-quarter and one-third time, and 15% continued working in a minimal capacity. Among those still employed after retirement, 44% were self-employed, 26% worked for private employers, and the remaining 30% worked for government, foundation, or education-related employers. Thus, even among men who "retired" from jobs, there was a considerable amount of continuity in paid employment after that retirement.

While a focus on single transitions is informative, it still does not provide the overall view of men's work in later life that interests us.

Some men slowly reduced their time until they were completely out of the labor force, but never defined any single transition as a retirement. Others "retired" but continued working full-time in similar types of jobs. To get a broader sense of work in later life, we defined five potential patterns of work and labor force exit.

For Terman men, the single most common pattern (35%) was gradual reduction in work time, applying to all who significantly reduced work time more than once but never left the labor force or who reduced work two or more times before fully retiring. The second most common pattern was a single exit out of the labor force, applying to 28% of the sample. Other patterns were sporadic movement in and out of the labor force (15%), no significant reduction in work time by the last survey (14%), and one partial reduction and then a full exit from the labor force (7%).

One measure of the validity of these patterns is a comparison of self-defined retirements with the overall patterns. While the two measures provide very different types of information about work lives, there should be some association between men's self-reported retirements and certain patterns. For example, 44% of the men who defined one transition as a retirement fit the pattern of a single exit from the labor force, while only 2% of the men who had no self-defined retirements fit this pattern. However, among those with one self-defined retirement, other patterns were possible: 29% had a gradual reduction in their work time and 17% retired or reduced their work time and later increased work time.

We expect other aspects of work, such as self-employment and occupation, to be associated with overall patterns of work in later life. Self-employed men are likely to have greater flexibility in choosing when and how they reduce their work. In many cases this flexibility may be coupled with greater economic pressure to continue working in the absence of an employer's pension plan, and both factors may make the self-employed more likely to reduce their work time gradually (Fuchs, 1982).

In part A of Figure 4.4 we confirm these expectations. In 1959, self-employed men were much more likely to reduce their work time gradually (52% versus 29%), while wage and salary workers were more apt to "retire" once (32% versus 15%). We note with interest that the two employment groups had an equal likelihood of continuing full-time work, and that men in wage and salary jobs in 1959 were more likely to retire and then return to the labor force (18% versus 8%). Probably many wage and salary earners in 1959 who did not reduce their hours or who gradually reduced them switched to self-employment at some later point in their work lives. Future analyses will be able to combine

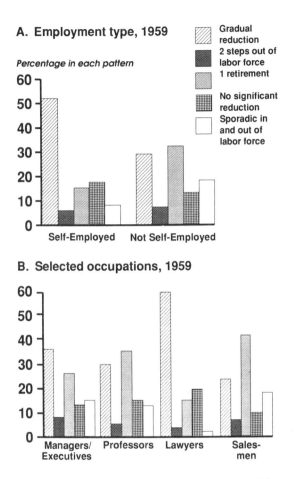

Figure 4.4. Patterns of Work in Later Life by Employment and Occupation

information on work-life patterns with that on sequences of transitions to explore these differences further.

Part B of Figure 4.4 compares work-life patterns across four 1959 occupations. A gradual reduction in work time was most common among lawyers, 80% of whom were self-employed, and least common among salesmen. Interestingly, managers/executives (37%) were as likely as professors (30%) to reduce work time gradually. Further analyses indicate that about a fourth of managers or executives in 1959 later changed careers, and an equal percentage worked as consultants in their later years. Both changes may allow a more gradual reduction in work than might be expected in a managerial position.

Percentages of men who exited the labor force once also vary significantly across occupations. Among salesmen, 42% fit the traditional pattern of a single retirement; at the other extreme, only 15% of lawyers retired in this way. Most surprising, a relatively high percentage of professors retired at one point (36%), but subsequent analyses suggest that many (61%) continued unpaid professional activities after reducing or stopping paid work. The other three work-life patterns are relatively similar across occupations, and differences, such as between lawyers and salesmen, mirror the corresponding differences in self-employment.

Overall, these comparisons suggest that our measures of work-life patterns, like those of health trajectories in Chapter 3, provide a unique, but not contradictory, view of work in later life. Consistent with previous research, our findings show that patterns of work correspond closely to the flexibility of an employment situation, thus supporting the validity of these new measures. At the same time, however, the measures document a dynamic view of work and retirement that enables us to address the complexity of men's work experiences in later life.

5. MEASURING HISTORICAL INFLUENCES

We have described up to this point a series of steps to be taken in the recasting of archival data so that they provide a better fit with research questions. In this concluding chapter, we focus on one of the more challenging problems in life-course study—extracting acceptable measures of historical influence from data archives. Problem formulation is critical to this task, and we underscore the need to incorporate historical influences in the question if they are of interest to the project. The fine detail of procedures in prior chapters has lower priority than conceptualization in this chapter.

An increased awareness of historical forces in human lives distinguishes the life-course revolution generally, but not in the priorities of data collection. For the most part, longitudinal studies have not eased the task of putting such awareness into practice. As noted in Chapter 2, the Terman Study ignored historical influences. Study members lived through the Great Depression and World War II during a formative time of education, family building, and career beginnings, yet the 1936-1950 follow-ups include not one question that directly focuses on either period of profound historical change. A more recent example of this blindness is the Panel Study of Income Dynamics, which began annual data collection on poverty issues in 1968 uninformed by the mobilization of disadvantaged young men for service in Vietnam.

With these limitations in mind, the Lewis Terman archive would seem to be the last place in which to investigate historical influences. How can one explore such influences when the original study director asked no direct questions about the times? One possible option involves the use of volunteered observations or reports on personal life. The Terman data archive includes an abundance of such information on most cases, from jottings on the edges of pages of closed-ended questions to tangential expansions of answers for open-ended questions and replies to letters from the Terman Study staff. Another option involves the use of collected data to measure, if only indirectly, a process or event of historical significance. Terman's occupational histories in relation to World War II are a case in point.

These histories are available on the oldest men during the 1930s and tell us something about the difficulties of career beginnings in hard times. However, most of the histories cover only the last half of the decade and thus miss the heart of the Great Depression. By comparison, the Terman staff collected occupational information for each year across the war era, and such data on military service or civilian employment are available on virtually all study members. The follow-ups in 1940, 1945, and 1950 are most important in providing this information.

The 1945 survey form reached some men while they were still under fire on the front lines. Terman received the following note appended to an information blank from the South Pacific: "I have been trying to kill some men today, and they in turn have been trying to kill me. In between these endeavors I have filled out your information blank. It's a very strange manner of living!" For these men in the service, the section on employment provided a place in which to describe changes in rank and location.

The occupational histories proved not to be useful to the concerns Terman's research group addressed, and "they were very difficult" to code in the 1970s and 1980s (Robert Sears, personal communication, 1987). Nonetheless, these data are among the core materials from which we fashioned an empirical approach to historical influence in men's lives. Letters from study members and their wives, plus reports from supervisors and fieldworkers, interview transcripts, and news clippings were also valuable. We benefited immensely from Sears's initial effort to extract all military and war material from the 1945 survey. Indeed, his coding effort provided a point of departure for us.

In this chapter we show how our preliminary efforts to assess the effects of wartime experience in the lives of the Terman men foundered on measures that proved to be inadequate in concept and operation. This discovery eventually led to a recoding decision on multiple aspects of wartime experience and to a serendipitous finding on home-front employment that led to a broader concept of war mobilization. The interplay of research question and archival data is clearly outlined by this investigative process.

Linking Historical Influences and Individual Lives

The Terman men came to military mobilization in World War II at a relatively late age, when they were launching adult careers in work and family. We identified two problem foci and their research questions on this transition and subsequent military experience. First was time of entry as a problem in men's lives. Both life-course theory and empirical findings (Elder, 1987) led us to expect more disruption and socioeconomic costs from the service for men who entered the war beyond age 30 or so. A second line of research questions addresses the stressfulness of wartime service and its life-course and health effects. Exposure to heavy combat increases the risk of posttraumatic stress symptoms as well as the likelihood of enduring relationships (Elder & Clipp, 1988).

A useful first step in historical analysis is the identification of birth cohorts and their relation to specific events and experiences. By locating study members in history, birth year enables us to relate lives to specific conditions and changes, such as the onset of World War II. But we do not know whether all men in a birth year were actually exposed to these conditions or changes. More information is needed. To some extent, then, the connection is imprecise, and causal links between social history and lives are generally left to the imagination. Nevertheless, grouping study members in birth cohorts provides a beginning and a point of departure.

It is a useful point of departure for the study of historical influence if the originating question concerns this influence. However, cohort studies are not necessarily motivated by this concern (Schaie, 1965). Indeed, the motivation for comparing successive birth cohorts of children or adults may stem from the assumption of developmental invariance. Environmental variations do not matter, at least in principle. With this in mind,

TABLE 5.1
Age of Terman Men by Birth Cohorts, by Historical Events

| Date | Event | Age by Birth Cohort | |
		1900-1909	1910-1920
1914-18	World War I	5-18	0-8
1921-1922	1920s depression	12-22	1-12
1923-1929	general economic boom	14-29	3-19
1929-1933	Great Depression onset	20-33	9-23
1933-1936	partial recovery	24-36	13-26
1937-1938	economic slump	28-38	17-28
1939-1940	start of war mobilization	30-40	19-30
1941-1943	major growth of armed forces and war industries	32-43	21-33
1945	end of World War II	36-45	25-35
1950-1953	Korean War	41-53	30-43
1957	peak of baby boom	48-57	37-47
1963-1973	Vietnam War	54-73	43-63
1973	end of postwar affluence	64-73	53-63

cohorts are viewed as samples that permit a test of this invariance or of the generalization boundaries (Baltes, Cornelius, & Nesselroade, 1979). Cohort sequential designs are typically used for this purpose.

By comparison, research questions on historical effects are prompted by a very different premise, that of developmental variation across cultures, social structures, and historical times. However, even when historical influence is substantively important, it may be operationalized as a period or cohort effect that provides no precise information as to the nature of the influence. We know that members of a particular cohort are not uniformly exposed to the historical record, and that experiential variations within specific cohorts are substantial.

Successive birth cohorts encounter the same historical conditions at different stages of life and so experience the events differently (Table 5.1). However, even members of a cohort do not all have the same historical experience. Not all members of the older and younger cohorts were exposed to severe hardship in the 1930s (we assume), and fewer than half served in World War II—50% of the younger men and 35% of the older men.

Membership in a specific birth cohort generally indicates a person's life stage at the time of change, such as the early 30s for men in the older Terman cohort when the United States entered the war. However, cohorts with a wide age range do not always locate people with enough precision. Age grading by the U.S. Selective Service enables us to achieve greater specificity for a study of war mobilization by using age at entry into the military service. Of the Terman men, 36% entered the armed forces before age 30, 42% were inducted at ages 30 through 32, and the remainder entered after age 32. These late entrants were mobilized at least 4 years beyond the median age for all servicemen during World War II. A majority of Terman veterans were inducted between the summers of 1942 and 1944 and demobilized about 4 years later.

From the computerized file of data on the Terman men, we managed to answer some general descriptive questions concerning the mobilized and the nonmobilized. Draft deferment policy changed as manpower needs soared during the middle of the war, but men with children were less likely to be drafted throughout the war than were childless married men and single men. We found a comparable differentiation among the Terman men, plus a tendency for later entrants to be better educated. This modest difference in education is not reflected by a corresponding IQ difference—all three entry groups are identical on IQ (Elder & Clipp, 1991). At the very least, men who entered after age 30 had more time in which to complete postgraduate education, compared with early entrants.

The recruits served in all branches, but most were in either the army or the navy (62% and 34%, respectively). About half of the men were officers at entry into formal duty, reflecting their high level of education and intellectual ability. This proportion increased to three-fourths by the time of demobilization. Nearly a fourth of the men served in the European theater; a third served in the Pacific theater. The remainder had mixed histories of location in the United States and abroad. One in four never served abroad.

Military service was only part of war mobilization during World War II, and did not include the majority of Terman men. With military service and home-front employment as elements of two historical boundaries for World War II, we defined the beginning of the nation's war mobilization in terms of enactment of the Selective Service Act on September 16, 1940, and extended it beyond the formal end of the war through the winding down of demobilization. Work histories on the Terman men enabled us to obtain premobilization employment between January and June 1940, and then information on postmobilization employment beginning during the winter of 1948. The second set of boundaries marks the formal entry of the United States into the war and the Japanese surrender on August 14, 1945 (Figure 5.1).

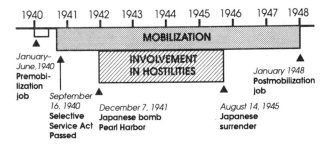

Figure 5.1. U.S. Mobilization and Involvement in Hostilities, World War II

In the course of archival work for the military service project, we began to see new possibilities for studying the impact of war mobilization on men who remained civilians and on men eventually mobilized for military duty at a later time. We envisioned ways of moving beyond mere evidence of civilian employment to evidence of war-related, home-front mobilization. The Terman life records show that some men on the home front were subject to greater stresses and opportunities than they would have experienced in peacetime. Yet manpower demands did not fall evenly on all. For some, the war meant long hours, radical occupational shifts, and cross-country relocation, while for others it produced relatively little change.

But what, we asked, are the defining features of war mobilization? With the collaboration of Andrew Workman from the Department of History at the University of North Carolina at Chapel Hill, we conceptualized *mobilization* as the organization of society for war in which the state strikes a balance between two processes—the commitment of a large part of a nation's production to the military and the continued provision for the civilian population (Fairchild & Grossman, 1959). Beyond this, the state must determine the degree to which normal social and economic processes should be controlled. To achieve goals in wartime, various agencies of the American state made explicit determinations as to what constituted mobilization. We chose to rely on relevant state decisions to delineate types of mobilization.

An extensive search of the administrative histories produced during the war led us to the policies of the War Manpower Commission and the Selective Service Administration to ascertain the importance of a man's activity to the war as a whole. We combined the general guidelines for local manpower committees and selective service boards with more explicit lists of essential activities to produce categories of war mobilization that could be applied to life-record data by trained coders. The two levels are as follows:

1. *Civilian activities necessary to war production:* Study members could be either (a) processing or producing ships, planes, tanks, guns and other machines, and instruments, articles, and materials directly used in conducting war or (b) government officials employed by war agencies or civilian employees employed by the armed forces. Examples include a scientist engaged in weapons research and an attorney on the War Production Board.
2. *Civilian activities supporting the war effort:* These were activities deemed essential for the national health, safety, or interest—other than war production—that supported the war effort, including occupations that produced for both civilian and military needs, such as mining and agriculture. Examples are textile manufacturer and police officer.

The utility of these analytic distinctions was affirmed by a review of individual cases and by the opportunity to place the wartime employment experience of men within the framework of war mobilization. Exploring home-front as well as military mobilization would result in a much broader concept of the original study and a rare opportunity to investigate these competing processes in men's lives.

To achieve this end, we had to devise serviceable measures of military experience from the follow-up of 1945-1946, a data collection not addressed to wartime experience in a comprehensive manner. For example, the men were not asked directly about their exposure to combat, although they often reported such experiences when answering other questions. During the early 1980s, Robert Sears, then director of the Terman Study, organized an effort to code the survey of 1945-1946 and gave personal attention to reports on wartime service. One of Sears's codes focused on exposure to combat in a general way, and we decided to see if we could use the measure to index wartime stress.

In addition to this source of information, Sears enabled us to collect retrospective information on wartime experiences during the 1986 follow-up. We were well aware of the memory limitations of such questions, but our doubts about wartime measures from the 1945-1946 follow-up encouraged this initiative. Drawing on a retrospective survey of Oakland Growth Study members in 1985, we added items to the 1986 follow-up on active duty, such as combat exposure, duration of combat service, use of the G.I. Bill, and appraisals of the personal impact of wartime service. Approximately 850 Terman men and women returned the survey form in 1986, among them more than 200 male veterans.

These 1986 data were not immediately available to us on tape for measuring combat experience, so we acquired copies of the survey forms to compare them with combat information from the 1945-1946 follow-up. We hoped to find substantial correspondence between reports of wartime combat at the two time points, a congruence that would enable us to include cases with reports of combat exposure at *either* time. This proved to be a fanciful aspiration in many respects. Our measures of combat experience in 1945-1946 and 1986 left much to be desired, and studies of the accuracy of retrospective accounts did not offer much empirical support. Nevertheless, we considered the comparison to be our best measurement strategy at the time. Could we emerge with confidence in a measure of combat experience?

We soon encountered dismaying results. First, the elderly sample of 1986 provided a relatively small cross-time sample, especially when we defined the sample in terms of evidence on combat in both data collections. Second, the correspondence between combat cases was too low to inspire confidence in either measurement. The 1986 report (asking respondents if they spent a week or more in combat) agreed with the 1945 index (exposed to combat or not) in only 38% of the cases. We discovered other discrepancies on dates of service entry and exit, rank at entry and exit, and even on branch of service.

To resolve the discrepancies on combat and other aspects of wartime service, we launched a review of materials for the problem cases in the project archive. Some inconsistencies were partially or completely resolved in this manner, particularly when letters and other supporting documents were available. However, more questions than answers were raised by the files on other cases. Based on these findings, we reluctantly concluded that a valid measure of combat experience could not be obtained from the 1945-1946 and 1986 data, alone or in combination. Moreover, we could not avoid doubts regarding the quality of measurement on other facets of the wartime experience.

Two options faced us at this point. We could restrict our proposed study of wartime experience to only those 1945-1946 data in which we had confidence, or we could develop suitable codes and apply them to an enriched file of life-history material on study members. To obtain such a file, we would need permission to photocopy all relevant material in the Terman archive at Stanford University. Developing a codebook and applying it to the data would follow. With no informed guidelines for estimates of time and cost, we chose the second option, in the belief that we could complete the task in six months. Grant resources did not cover the travel expense or coding enterprise itself, as we anticipated it at the time. But they were even less sufficient to cover the actual project as it unfolded, including four trips to Stanford of about two weeks each and nearly a full year of coding.

Nevertheless, we realized that recasting the Terman archive for the purposes of this study would enable us to do the proposed research and to do it better than we thought we could during the planning stage. This was so because new coding on combat experiences made more sense when expanded to a multifaceted account of wartime experiences in the context of men's lifetime military service. From the very beginning this account included both military and home-front mobilization. Men mobilized for military service typically came from employment of some kind, and we viewed this work experience, very loosely, as part of home-front mobilization.

A study of this kind calls for detailed coding of occupations during the war and its demobilization phase. We were familiar with the Terman data on work, and we knew that the disruption and disorder of life in wartime could substantially diminish the completeness and overall quality of work histories across the war years. Nevertheless, the Terman data on occupational change stand at the center of the individual files, generously supplemented by letters to and from the Terman staff, career advice from Terman, and news clippings.

Any reworking of the wartime occupational data would clearly add to the burden of the recasting effort for the military study, yet we could also achieve economies of scale by linking the two studies. They are complementary in their research on different aspects of war mobilization, and both required the preparation of codebooks and their application to data by trained coders. The same team of coders could be trained for the two recasting efforts. With these considerations in mind, we describe the development of the new codes and their application.

New Codes for Research Questions

As we turn to the task of creating new codes for our questions on the effects of military and home-front war mobilization, it is useful to recognize the distinctive nature of the questions themselves. Our research on

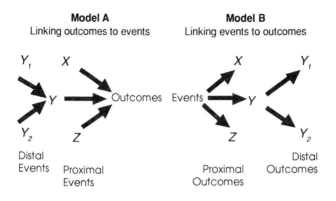

Figure 5.2. Studying Social Change in the Life Course: Two Models

historical influences begins with the historical process or condition and branches out to multiple outcomes. The central question focuses on the process by which social change and times make a difference in the life course. In the case of war mobilization, we ask how it changes the life situations of those caught up in the process. Knowledge of these effects provides clues on plausible life-course variations and outcomes.

The starting point in research questions that assume this perspective involves an understanding of the historical process. What is the nature of military service and home-front mobilization, and how did it influence the men involved? Other research questions begin with a particular outcome of the individual and ask what factors influence it. Not all factors involve the environment, so research with this design usually has very little to say about environmental effects or social change. When research views the social environment from the vantage of the developing individual in context, it is unlikely to develop the full implications of a changing social system for the individual.

Figure 5.2 provides a schematic representation of the two types of questions. Model A starts with the individual and works back to the environment, whereas Model B begins with an environmental change and traces its multiple effects across the life course. Model B represents the perspective we have employed in archival research on military service and home-front mobilization. In developing appropriate codes for this line of work, we focused on wartime combat in the military study, with some attention to other aspects of the service experience. In the home-front study, work experience during the war became the target of our efforts in developing more suitable codes. We began with conceptual notions about combat experience and their correspondence with the Terman archival data, then turned to ways of thinking about and measuring work experience during World War II.

CODING WARTIME EXPERIENCE

From social and developmental perspectives, the service experience has at least three distinct features:

1. Military experience severs past experience from considerations of the present, separating recruits from family and community, thus curtailing the influence of prior life histories and obligations.
2. Time in the service represents a legitimate time-out from age-graded career and responsibilities, a time for reassessment and new considerations.
3. Military duty tends to broaden the range of personal experiences, from social acquaintances to new places and opportunities.

Although greater social independence, a broader range of experiences, and a time-out from career pressures do not cover all relevant features of World War II mobilization, together they define a common culture for men who served. Within this framework, exposure to combat is one of three key variables of wartime experience as we conceptualize it. The others are the timing of entry (well measured in the original data) and social ties with service mates (covered in the 1986 Terman follow-up).

Theoretical accounts of wartime experience have evolved from single dimensions (e.g., duration of exposure) in World War II studies to multiple dimensions in research on Vietnam veterans. Samuel Stouffer's pioneering study of American soldiers in World War II (Stouffer et al., 1949) relied mainly on a question about exposure to combat. By comparison, studies of Vietnam veterans have used a more differentiated theory and measurement model to capture the diversity of wartime stress. Robert Laufer (1985), for example, explored three dimensions of war stress that bear on subsequent symptomatology and behavioral problems: (a) exposure to life-threatening situations, (b) exposure to abusive violence, and (c) participation in episodes of abusive violence.

Our conceptual and measurement approach borrowed from this line of thinking by assuming that combat experience is defined by exposure to the dying, wounded, and dead, and to incoming and outgoing gunfire.

Combat duration is relevant to fire and death experiences by increasing their probability of occurrence. With these distinctions in mind, we reviewed the files on approximately 30 Terman men who served in the military. This inventory provided an empirical map of men's wartime experience as expressed in the 1945-1946 and 1950 follow-up materials, related letters, and reports. Catherine Cross (project manager) and two highly skilled coders from the Carolina Population Center played central roles in this survey and in the construction of a military service codebook with six sections:

1. *Lifetime military and military-related experiences:* veteran status and type; service before, during, and after World War II; entry and exit information; service career, branch, and unit; medals and education linked to the service (e.g., ROTC, GI Bill)

2. *Overseas experience before World War II or U.S. involvement:* duty for government, volunteer agency

3. *Home-front experience during World War II:* deferments, conscientious objector status, service with government

4. *Wartime stress:* combat duration in weeks and months; experience of firing at the enemy and of being fired upon; exposure to wounded and dead (Allies and enemy); experiences of being wounded, held in a prisoner of war camp, and missing in action (also identified men killed in action, 3% of the total sample)

5. *Postwar experiences linked to the war:* civil administration duties during military occupation, medical care for Allied wounded, and medical evaluation for repatriation or emigration

6. *Domestic exposure to care of American wounded and the dying:* experience of medical personnel in the sample, separated from those on the front line

Because of the complexity of the coding operation, we recruited well-educated coders and trained them in basic military history, life-course methodology, and specific coding procedures. We first constructed summary sheets on the men's military history through careful review of the entire data file on study members, since the information was not systematically ordered on the original survey forms. Further, a substantial part of the information came from sundry letters and news clippings. With an initial draft of the codebook in hand, Cross and the coders applied it to a set of cases. Codesheets were then checked and disparities discussed. Five such trials each led to revisions in the codes that in turn produced an improved fit with the data.

TABLE 5.2

Active Duty and Combat Experience of Terman Men During World
War II, in Percentages

	Rank at Exit		
Active Duty Experiences	Officer	Enlisted	Total
All veterans			N = 343
World War II active duty			96
World War II veterans	N = 230	N = 71	N = 329
served overseas	60	58	58
served in combat theater	47	39	43
was fired on/fired at enemy	27	23	25
saw Allied/enemy wounded or killed	35	25	31
combat			
yes	53	41	48
no	31	35	30
cannot be determined	17	24	22
World War II veterans serving			
in combat theater	N = 108	N = 28	N = 142
was fired on/fired at enemy	57	57	57
saw Allied/enemy wounded or killed	66	61	64
wounded in action	14	18	15
MIA or POW	2	7	3
killed in action	1	7	3

This procedure entailed a thorough review of all materials for a particular case over the life course, with attention to event chronology. Coders
were to extract relevant clues and data from a large body of material, to
make judgments based on these clues, and to identify potential trouble
spots in the data and coding scheme. The painstaking work in fitting the
codebook to the data paid off handsomely in the actual coding process. At
the halfway mark in coding, we had completed reliability checks on 20%
of the cases, or about 85 men. The checks were restricted to the war stress
measures, since this domain was most important in our work and required
the highest levels of coder expertise in judgment. The total average
intercoder reliability on these variables was 98% at the mid-point and
remained above 96% over the entire project.

In Table 5.2 we use the resulting codes to portray combat experience
in the Terman sample. Three of five World War II veterans served
overseas, a figure that does not vary by rank at demobilization. A large
percentage of the overseas veterans served in a combat theater with

some exposure to gunfire and death. Most veterans who served in a combat zone show evidence of involvement in heavy combat. For our study, we defined *heavy combat* in terms of exposure to gunfire and death or dying. All men who were wounded or declared missing in action, prisoners of war, or killed in action were also assigned to this category. Of the Terman veterans, 26% saw heavy combat, 56% had no evidence of combat, and 18% were assigned to light combat.

Examples of heavy combat include a captain in the Railsplitters Company (Leinbaugh & Campbell, 1985) who fought in the Battle of the Bulge and a navy battalion executive officer who served in four amphibious assaults, including Okinawa and Kwajalein. After four and a half years in the navy, he observed, "I have not been wounded, although I have had numerous 'close ones' in the course of 152 days of combat with the Japs." Another officer served 190 days on the front line after the Normandy invasion, including the Battle of the Bulge. Terman noted in 1954 that only 12 mates survived in the captain's military unit—he "considers himself fortunate."

Consistent with the literature, we find that heavy combat veterans were recruited disproportionately from men who entered in the youngest age category. Heavy combat increased the risk of impaired emotional health after the war primarily among men who ranked below average on self-confidence and self-esteem before the war, and it markedly increased memories of the war as a highly influential experience in life among men in old age (Elder & Clipp, 1991). Though combat is less common among late entrants in the Terman sample, and their prewar health equaled that of the early entrants, we find that late mobilization placed an unusual number at risk of postwar physical decline. All of these initial effects have consequences for the later years of health and retirement, and thus begin to suggest valuable returns from our recasting efforts on health, late-life careers, and wartime experience.

Our original decision to develop new codes on wartime experience led to a greatly enlarged set of variables for analysis that extends well beyond combat. For the first time, we have information on the life experiences men brought to the Second World War, and can show that military influences continued for some men well after the end of hostilities. The battery of new codes enables us to address our original questions with measurements that warrant confidence. However, military service is only part of war mobilization, and most of the Terman men remained at work on the home front. We turn now to our efforts to develop occupational codes for these men.

TABLE 5.3

Codes for Work Experience in War Years

---

1. Job type
   A. employer classification—sector of economy (private, government)
   B. industrial sector—manufacturing, finance, communication, etc.
   C. occupation of worker
   D. supervision (Does individual manage people?)
   E. time—proportion of day worked, seasonality of work, etc.
   F. mobilization—whether mobilized or not
2. Life changes
   A. job change
   B. employer change
3. Dates
   Includes beginning month and year and ending month and year for each job in mobilization period

---

CODING HOME-FRONT MOBILIZATION

Efforts to measure the military experience of the Terman men led to the realization that we could also investigate home-front mobilization and related occupational experience. Nearly 500 Terman men remained civilians for the entire war period, and a substantial number of the men who entered the service spent time in the civilian work force. Occupational histories during the years of war mobilization (see Figure 5.1) proved to be sufficiently detailed to let us chart careers across this period and classify each job in the occupational sequence on mobilization status and other defining characteristics.

Initial reviews of the work histories suggested that we could identify men directly involved in war-related work from descriptions of their jobs and employers, and that we might be able to estimate life changes due to mobilization from evidence of change in work life, such as switches in jobs, occupations, and employment sector; and in work characteristics, from total hours at work per day and week to supervisory responsibility and geographic mobility. Keeping in mind our interest in life-course change and the conceptual possibilities of work-history information, we decided to develop measurement procedures for six attributes of a job (Table 5.3).

The distinction between employment by private business and employment by government is critical in time of war mobilization. A branch manager of a local War Production Board would be coded "federal government"; a manager for Lockheed qualifies as "private business." The industrial sector category enables us to identify occupational changes involving a change in industry. For guidelines, we relied on the 1980 U.S. Census procedures for coding industry and occupation, a third attribute. Because of the similarity of the Terman surveys to census forms, we found the Census Bureau's system comprehensive and manageable to apply.

In times of labor shortage, opportunities for advancement and managerial responsibility increase, hence the code for supervision. Wartime production demands tend to lead to increased work hours of employees, so we included a code for time. The sixth job attribute, war mobilization, is one of the most important for our purposes, and we constructed codes from government policy mandates that distinguish three main categories: nonmobilized, directly mobilized, and indirectly mobilized.

We decided that, in addition to these job attributes, the coding operation should determine whether job and employer changes had occurred by drawing on all available information from the job attributes above and related data. In contemporary surveys, job and employer changes could be determined quantitatively. However, archival data from long-past surveys are uneven across codes and respondents in amount and quality of data. The data situation calls for coders' very best judgment on whether a job or employer change has occurred. Only primary jobs were compared to determine job stability or change. Coders were instructed to add the month and year of entry and exit each time they noted a change. This information enables us to use event history analyses on the process of war mobilization.

The coding form is designed to capture all job changes for the war period, which we define as between September 1940 and December 1947, as well as a pre- and postmobilization job on either end of this interval. For our purposes, *premobilization* refers to the last job held between January and June 1940, and *postmobilization* to the job held in January 1948. We view 1940 employment as a baseline for assessing work-life changes across the war years. An example is a Terman man who was an assistant professor in a West Coast university before mobilization. The codesheet indicates that he taught foreign relations full-time and supervised no one. During mobilization, he did social science research for the federal government in a national security agency, clearly a shift from indirectly mobilized employment to work directly concerned with fighting the war. By war's end, he had moved to a high administrative position, from which he took a job as a high-level administrator with a private philanthropic foundation—a job he kept in the postmobilization stage.

The same two coders who coded military service were hired for the home-front project. They were well acquainted with the Terman data and had substantial training in archival coding procedures. The coders and project managers (Workman, Cross) applied the first draft of the codebook to materials in the 1940, 1945, and 1950 follow-ups—mainly survey forms, letters, and clippings. Ratings were assembled and compared so that disparities could be discussed in conference. After three more rounds of application and revision, each showing high levels of agreement, we began final coding.

All nonveterans were coded first, because they had the most complete work histories across the war years. At the end of this part of the project, we had achieved substantial agreement across all but one code—residential change. War mobilization is coupled with an unusual amount of residential change, and we hoped to obtain the numbers and types of such changes. Unfortunately, data on residence proved to be too vague to support reliable codes. Two procedures were used to determine coder agreement. First, we wanted to know the extent of agreement between coders on jobs for a study member—whether coders were making adjustments about the same job or not. The second appraisal focused on job attributes such as supervision, time schedule, and mobilization status. Using percentage agreement, we achieved an average agreement of 94 for all jobs and job attributes; none received an average agreement of less than 90.

As we follow the Terman men across the war years, the percentage in military uniform increased dramatically, especially between 1942 and 1943, and so also did the percentage of men who were engaged in civilian activities deemed essential to war production—an indication of direct mobilization (Figure 5.3). Though less than a fifth of the Terman men were involved in such activity during the war, the percentage was double what it was in 1941. Indirectly mobilized men had less priority for continuing their employment, and a substantial number were involved in the military and essential work for the war effort by the end of 1945.

Younger men were more likely than older men to be mobilized directly, either in the military or in home-front war-related activities (Figure 5.4). Military duty is a young person's activity, as defined by society, but necessary home-front work on behalf of the war effort also seemed to favor younger men. This selection may reflect the life stage of younger men who were in the market for greater opportunities; it may

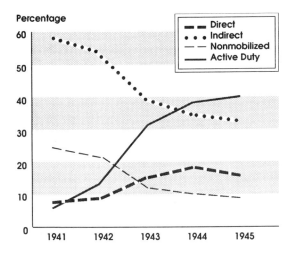

Figure 5.3. Percentage of Military and Home-Front Mobilization of Terman Men, 1941-1945

also reflect family and career barriers to life-course change among the older men. Younger men are more open to residential change and have less to lose in giving up one job for another that seems more promising. Manpower pressures from the top may also have favored the selection of highly educated younger men. In any case, any calculation of life-course change must take into account prewar employment history and the specific characteristics of occupations. These considerations will inform our agenda as we investigate the dual effects of military and home-front mobilization on men's lives.

Conclusion

Though social scientists generally acknowledge the profound role of historical influences in shaping human lives, they have much distance to travel in translating this knowledge into practice. The early longitudinal studies were uninformed on ways of relating a changing social world to life patterns, and more contemporary studies have made little progress along these lines. Major longitudinal studies are still designed without attention to the historical record, and some researchers still seem to believe that history is only a backdrop to their studies.

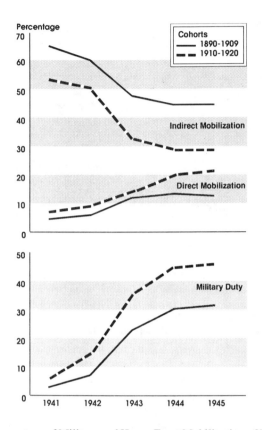

Figure 5.4. Percentage of Military and Home-Front Mobilization of Terman Men by Cohort, 1941-1945

With these considerations in mind, *a most important step toward the life-course study of historical influences involves their incorporation in the statement of a research question.* Historical questions do not focus research on historical effects. Moreover, they do not lead to the collection of data on historical effects or to the selection of data archives with possibilities for historical analyses. In setting up his study, Lewis Terman did not have historical or environmental effects in mind, so he failed to ask a single question about the Great Depression or World War II in life experience. Historically relevant data were collected over the years in this project, but mainly individually, through letters and news clippings. By recasting these and other data in the Terman files to produce codes on historical circumstances and experience, we obtained measures of military and home-front mobilization for the Terman men.

The qualitative and quantitative data in the Terman files made our construction of new codes possible. Survey data with structured, closed-end questions and no open-ended questions do not provide the opportunity for such recasting, and a large proportion of current longitudinal studies fit this limited model. The older longitudinal studies, by contrast, generally collected rich qualitative materials along with the quantitative data, and provide rare opportunities to study lives in a rapidly changing society. Our approach to the reworking of the Terman data was developed from such efforts with the Oakland and Berkeley Guidance Study data, and we hope it will have applications in other studies as well.

APPENDIX:
THE HENRY A. MURRAY RESEARCH CENTER
OF RADCLIFFE COLLEGE

As described in the *Inventory of Longitudinal Studies in the Social Sciences* (Young et al., 1991), the Henry A. Murray Research Center of Radcliffe College, a Center for the Study of Lives, was established in 1976 as a national repository for data in the fields of psychology, psychiatry, sociology, anthropology, economics, political science, and education. The center archives original subject records plus coded, machine-readable data. The original records often include transcripts of thorough interviews, behavioral observations, responses to projective tests, and other information useful for secondary analysis. Having access to such ancillary material makes it possible for researchers to restructure the subject records and mitigates the degree to which they are locked into the theoretical assumptions under which the data were collected. Interested persons may request a copy of the *Guide to the Data Resources,* which provides information on nearly 200 data sets, and the *Index to the Guide,* which lists methods of data collection and content areas of each. Contact Anne Colby, Ph.D., Director, Henry A. Murray Research Center of Radcliffe College, 10 Garden Street, Cambridge, MA 02138; (617) 495-8140.

REFERENCES

ALLPORT, G. W. (1942) The Use of Personal Documents in Psychological Science. New York: Social Science Research Council.

BAILEY, K. D. (1978) Methods of Social Research. New York: Free Press.

BALTES, P. B., CORNELIUS, S. W., and NESSELROADE, J. R. (1979) "Cohort effects in developmental psychology," pp. 61-87 in J. R. Nesselroade and P. B. Baltes (eds.) Longitudinal Research in the Study of Behavior and Development. New York: Academic.

BARTKO, J. J. (1966) "The intraclass correlation coefficient as a measure of reliability." Psychological Reports 19: 3-11.

BOLLEN, K. A. (1989) Structural Equations With Latent Variables. New York: John Wiley.

BROOKS-GUNN, J., PHELPS, E., and ELDER, G. H., Jr. (1991) "Studying lives through time: Secondary data analyses in developmental psychology." Developmental Psychology 27: 899-910.

BURDOCK, E. I., FLEISS, J. L., and HARDESTY, A. S. (1963) "A new view of inter-observer agreement." Personnel Psychology 16: 373-384.

CAMPBELL, R. T., and O'RAND, A. M. (1988) "Settings and sequences: The heuristics of aging research," pp. 58-79 in J. E. Birren and V. L. Bengtson (eds.) Emergent Theories of Aging. New York: Springer.

COHEN, J. (1968) "Weighted kappa: Nominal scale agreement with provision for scaled disagreement or partial credit." Psychological Bulletin 70: 213-220.

DUNCAN, G. J., with COE, R. D., CORCORAN, M. E., HILL, M. S., HOFFMAN, S. C., and MORGAN, J. N. (1984) Years of Poverty, Years of Plenty: The Changing Economic Fortunes of American Workers and Families. Ann Arbor, MI: Institute for Social Research.

DUNCAN, G. J., and MORGAN, N. J. (1985) "The panel study of income dynamics," pp. 50-71 in G. H. Elder, Jr. (ed.) Life Course Dynamics: Trajectories and Transitions, 1968-1980. Ithaca, NY: Cornell University Press.

EBEL, R. L. (1951) "Estimation of the reliability of ratings." Psychometrika 16: 407-424.

EICHORN, D. H., CLAUSEN, J. A., HAAN, N., HONZIK, M. P., and MUSSEN, P. H. (eds.) (1981) Present and Past in Middle Life. New York: Academic Press.

ELDER, G. H., Jr. (1974) Children of the Great Depression: Social Change in Life Experience. Chicago: University of Chicago Press.

ELDER, G. H., Jr. (1979) "Historical change in life patterns and personality," pp. 117-159 in P. B. Baltes and O. G. Brim, Jr. (eds.) Life-Span Development and Behavior (vol. 2). New York: Academic Press.

ELDER, G. H., Jr. (1985) "Perspectives on the life course," pp. 23-49 in G. H. Elder, Jr. (ed.) Life Course Dynamics: Trajectories and Transitions, 1968-1980. Ithaca, NY: Cornell University Press.

ELDER, G. H., Jr. (1986) "Military times and turning points in men's lives." Developmental Psychology 22: 233-245.

ELDER, G. H., Jr. (1987) "War mobilization and the life course: A cohort of World War II veterans." Sociological Forum 2: 449-472.

ELDER, G. H., Jr. (1992) "Studying women's lives: Research questions, strategies and lessons," in S. Powers (ed.) Studying Women's Lives: The Use of Archival Data. New Haven, CT: Yale University Press.

ELDER, G. H., Jr., CASPI, A., and DOWNEY, G. (1986) "Problem behavior and family relationships: Life course and intergenerational themes," pp. 293-340 in A. B. Sørensen, F. E. Weinert, and L. R. Sherrod (eds.), Human Development and the Life Course: Multidisciplinary Perspectives. Hillsdale, NJ: Lawrence Erlbaum.

ELDER, G. H., Jr., and CLIPP, E. C. (1988) "Wartime losses and social bonding: Influences across 40 years in men's lives." Psychiatry 51: 177-198.

ELDER, G. H., Jr., and CLIPP, E. C. (1991) "War's legacy in men's lives." Presented at the annual meetings of the Gerontological Society, San Francisco.

FAIRCHILD, B., and GROSSMAN, J. (1959) The Army and Industrial Manpower. Washington, DC: Department of the Army, Office of the Chief of Military History.

FEATHERMAN, D. L., and LERNER, R. M. (1985) "Ontogenesis and sociogenesis: Problematics for theory and research about development and socialization across the lifespan." American Sociological Review 50: 659-676.

FILLENBAUM, G. G., and MADDOX, G. L. (1974) "Work after retirement: An investigation into some psychologically relevant variables." Gerontologist 14: 418-424.

FLEISS, J. L. (1971) "Measuring nominal scale agreement among many raters." Psychological Bulletin 76: 378-382.

FLEISS, J. L. (1973) Statistical Methods for Rates and Proportions. New York: John Wiley.

FREEDMAN, D., THORNTON, A., CAMBURN, D., ALWIN, D., and YOUNG-DeMARCO, L. (1988) "The life history calendar: A technique for collecting retrospective data." Sociological Methodology 18: 37-68.

FUCHS, V. R. (1982) "Self-employment and labor force participation of older males." Journal of Human Resources 17: 339-357.

GUSTMAN, A. L., and STEINMEIER, T. L. (1984) "Partial retirement and the analysis of retirement behavior." Industrial and Labor Relations Review 37: 403-415.

HAREVEN, T. K. (1982) Family Time and Industrial Time: The Relationship Between the Family and Work in a New England Industrial Community. Cambridge: Cambridge University Press.

HOGAN, D. P. (1981) Transitions and Social Change: The Early Lives of American Men. New York: Academic Press.

HONIG, M., and HANOCH, G. (1985) "Partial retirement as a separate mode of retirement behavior." Journal of Human Resources 20: 21-46.

HYMAN, H. H. (1972) Secondary Analysis of Sample Surveys: Principles, Procedure, and Potentialities. New York: John Wiley.

IDLER, E., and KASL, S. (1991) "Health perceptions and survival: Do global evaluations of health status really predict mortality?" Journal of Gerontology: Social Science 46: 55-65.

JONES, M. C., BAYLEY, N., MacFARLANE, J. W., and HONZIK, M. P. (eds.) (1971) The Course of Human Development: Selected Papers from the Longitudinal Studies, Institute of Human Development, the University of California, Berkeley. Waltham, MA: Xerox College Publishing.

86

LANDIS, J. R., and KOCH, G. G. (1977) "The measure of observer agreement for categorical data." Biometrics 33: 159-174.

LAUB, J. H. (1991) "Reconstructing the Gluecks' *Unraveling Juvenile Delinquency* data." Presented at the workshop, Working With Longitudinal Data: New Questions for Old Data, Cambridge, MA.

LAUFER, R. S. (1985) "War trauma and human development: The Viet Nam experience," pp. 31-55 in S. M. Sonnenberg, A. S. Blank, Jr., and J. A. Talbot (eds.) The Trauma of War: Stress and Recovery in Viet Nam Veterans. Washington, DC: American Psychiatric Press.

LEINBAUGH, H. P., and CAMPBELL, J. D. (1985) The Men of Company K: The Autobiography of a World War II Rifle Company. New York: William Morrow.

LIGHT, R. J. (1971) "Measures of response agreement for qualitative data: Some generalizations and alternatives." Psychological Bulletin 76: 365-377.

LINN, B. S., LINN, M. W., and GUREL, L. (1968) "Cumulative illness rating scale." Journal of the American Geriatrics Society 16: 622-626.

MADDOX, G. L., and DOUGLASS, E. B. (1973) "Self-assessment of health: A longitudinal study of elderly subjects." Journal of Health and Social Behavior 14: 87-93.

MAYER, K. U., and TUMA, N. B. (eds.). (1990) Event History Analysis in Life Course Research. Madison: University of Wisconsin Press.

McLANAHAN, S. S., and SØRENSEN, A. B. (1985) "Life events and psychological well-being over the life course," pp. 217-238 in G. H. Elder, Jr. (ed.) Life Course Dynamics: Trajectories and Transitions, 1968-1980. Ithaca, NY: Cornell University Press.

MERTON, R. K. (1959) "Notes on problem-finding in sociology," pp. ix-xxxiv in R. K. Merton, L. Broom, and L. S. Cottrell, Jr. (eds.) Sociology Today: Problems and Prospects. New York: Basic Books.

MERTON, R. K. (1968) Social Theory and Social Structure (enl. ed.). New York: Free Press.

MINTON, H. L. (1988a) "Charting life history: Lewis M. Terman's study of the gifted," pp. 138-162 in J. G. Morawski (ed.) The Rise of Experimentation in American Psychology. New Haven, CT: Yale University Press.

MINTON, H. L. (1988b) Lewis M. Terman: Pioneer in Psychological Testing. New York: New York University Press.

MYERS, D. A. (1991) "Work after cessation of career job." Journal of Gerontology: Social Sciences 46: 93-102.

RILEY, M. W., JOHNSON, M. E., and FONER, A. (1972) Aging and Society, Vol. 3: A Sociology of Age Stratification. New York: Russell Sage Foundation.

ROBINSON, W. S. (1957) "The statistical measure of agreement." American Sociological Review 22: 17-25.

RYDER, N. B. (1965) "The cohort as a concept in the study of social change." American Sociological Review 30: 843-861.

SCHAIE, K. W. (1965) "A general model for the study of developmental problems." Psychological Bulletin 64: 94-107.

SPITZER, R. L., COHEN, J., FLEISS, J. L., and ENDICOTT, J. (1967) "Quantification of agreement in psychiatric diagnosis." Archives of General Psychiatry 17: 83-87.

STOUFFER, S. A., LUMSDAINE, A. A., LUMSDAINE, M. H., WILLIAMS, R. M., Jr., SMITH, M. B., JANIS, I. L., STAR, S. A., and COTTRELL, L. S., Jr. (1949) The American Soldier (2 vols.). Princeton, NJ: Princeton University Press.

TERMAN, L. M., with the assistance of others (1925) Genetic Studies of Genius, Vol. 1: Mental and Physical Traits of a Thousand Gifted Children. Stanford, CA: Stanford University Press.

TERMAN, L. M., and ODEN, M. H. (1959) Genetic Studies of Genius, Vol. 5: The Gifted Group at Mid-Life: Thirty-Five Years of Follow-Up of the Superior Child. Stanford, CA: Stanford University Press.

TESCH, R. (1990) Qualitative Research: Analysis Types and Software Tools. New York: Falmer.

THOMAS, W. I., and ZNANIECKI, F. (1918-1920) The Polish Peasant in Europe and America. Boston: R. G. Badger/Gorham.

TUMA, N. B., and HANNAN, M. T. (1984) Social Dynamics: Models and Methods. Orlando, FL: Academic Press.

VOLKART, E. H. (1951) Social Behavior and Personality: Contributions of W. I. Thomas to Theory and Social Research. New York: Social Science Research Council.

WILENSKY, H. L. (1961) "Orderly careers and social participation: The impact of work history on the social integration in the middle mass." American Sociological Review 26: 521-539.

YOUNG, C. H., SAVELA, K. L., and PHELPS, E. (1991) Inventory of Longitudinal Studies in the Social Sciences. Newbury Park, CA: Sage.

ABOUT THE AUTHORS

GLEN H. ELDER, Jr., is Howard W. Odum Distinguished Professor of Sociology and Research Professor of Psychology at the University of North Carolina at Chapel Hill, where he directs the Social Change Project on life-course studies and teaches in this field. His use of longitudinal data archives began in the early 1960s at the University of California, Berkeley, and he has continued such work up to the present through faculty appointments at Cornell and UNC at Chapel Hill.

ELIZA K. PAVALKO is Assistant Professor of Sociology at Indiana University. Her primary interests are in health, aging, and work, and she is currently using the Terman archives to examine how patterns of work in mid- and later life influence men's longevity.

ELIZABETH C. CLIPP is Research Assistant Professor of Medicine and Clinical Assistant Professor of Nursing at Duke University Medical Center, and Nurse Researcher at the Geriatric Research, Education and Clinical Center at the Durham Veterans Administration Medical Center. Her current research involves issues related to patterns of health in aging and quality of life in chronic illness.

Quantitative Applications in the Social Sciences

A SAGE UNIVERSITY PAPER SERIES

$13.95 each

To order, please use order form on the next page.

Quantitative Applications in the Social Sciences

A SAGE UNIVERSITY PAPER SERIES

$13.95 each

SAGE PUBLICATIONS, INC.
P.O. BOX 5084
THOUSAND OAKS, CALIFORNIA 91359-9924

Place
Stamp
here